PENGUIN BOOKS

THE FEDERALIST PAPERS

ALEXANDER HAMILTON was born in the British West Indian island of Nevis sometime between 1755 and 1757. During the Revolutionary War, he was captain of a New York artillery company and soon thereafter was promoted to lieutenant colonel, serving as George Washington's secretary and aide-de-camp. He was a delegate to the Constitutional Convention of 1787 from New York. Following that convention, he organized the writing of *The Federalist* essays, enlisting John Jay and James Madison in the effort. From 1789 to 1795 he served as America's first secretary of the Treasury. A growing animosity between Hamilton and his longtime New York political rival Aaron Burr culminated in a duel between the two men in 1804. Hamilton was fatally shot and died the day after their encounter.

JAMES MADISON is frequently referred to as "the father of the Constitution" because of the important role he played in the drafting of the US Constitution during the Constitutional Convention in Philadelphia during the summer of 1787. He also played a key role in drafting the Bill of Rights in the First Federal Congress in 1789. He later served as secretary of state under Thomas Jefferson, and succeeded Jefferson as president, serving two terms in that office and overseeing the United States victory over Great Britain in the War of 1812. He was the last Founding Father to die, in 1836, in Montpelier, Virginia.

JOHN JAY was a consistent voice for reconciliation with Great Britain in the Continental Congress. While he did not sign the Declaration of Independence, he later worked to secure support for independence in his home state of New York. He was an influential member of the peace delegation that negotiated the treaty of peace with Great Britain, ending the Revolutionary War. Recruited by Alexander Hamilton to write essays for *The Federalist*, his effort was hampered by illness.

Jay later served as the first chief justice of the Supreme Court. He retired from the Supreme Court in 1795 and served as governor of New York for six years before retiring to a farm for the last twenty-seven years of his life.

RICHARD BEEMAN, the John Welsh Centenniel Professor of History Emeritus at the University of Pennsylvania, has previously served as the chair of the Department of History, associate dean in Penn's School of Arts and Sciences, and dean of the College of Arts of Sciences. He serves as a trustee of the National Constitution Center and on the center's executive committee. The author of seven previous books, among them *The Penguin Guide to the United States Constitution* and *Plain, Honest Men: The Making of the American Constitution*, Professor Beeman has received numerous grants and awards, including fellowships from the National Endowment for the Humanities, the Rockefeller Foundation, the Institute for Advanced Study at Princeton, and the Huntington Library. His biography of Patrick Henry was a finalist for the National Book Award.

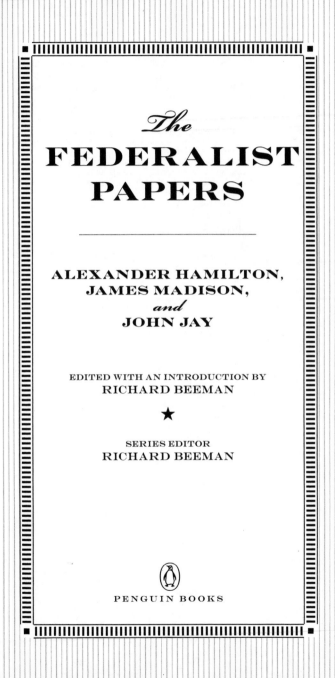

The FEDERALIST PAPERS

ALEXANDER HAMILTON,
JAMES MADISON,
and
JOHN JAY

EDITED WITH AN INTRODUCTION BY
RICHARD BEEMAN

★

SERIES EDITOR
RICHARD BEEMAN

PENGUIN BOOKS

PENGUIN BOOKS
Published by the Penguin Group
Penguin Group (USA) Inc., 375 Hudson Street, New York, New York 10014, U.S.A.
Penguin Group (Canada), 90 Eglinton Avenue East, Suite 700, Toronto, Ontario,
Canada M4P 2Y3 (a division of Pearson Penguin Canada Inc.)
Penguin Books Ltd, 80 Strand, London WC2R 0RL, England
Penguin Ireland, 25 St Stephen's Green, Dublin 2, Ireland
(a division of Penguin Books Ltd)
Penguin Group (Australia), 250 Camberwell Road, Camberwell, Victoria 3124,
Australia (a division of Pearson Australia Group Pty Ltd)
Penguin Books India Pvt Ltd, 11 Community Centre,
Panchsheel Park, New Delhi - 110 017, India
Penguin Group (NZ), 67 Apollo Drive, Rosedale, Auckland 0632, New Zealand
(a division of Pearson New Zealand Ltd)
Penguin Books (South Africa) (Pty) Ltd, 24 Sturdee Avenue, Rosebank,
Johannesburg 2196, South Africa

Penguin Books Ltd, Registered Offices:
80 Strand, London WC2R 0RL, England

This edition first published in Penguin Books 2012

13   15   17   19   20   18   16   14

Book introduction and series introduction copyright © Richard Beeman, 2012
All rights reserved

No copyright is claimed on works of the United States Government.

LIBRARY OF CONGRESS CATALOGING IN PUBLICATION DATA
Federalist.
The Federalist papers / Alexander Hamilton, James Madison, and John Jay;
edited with an introduction by Richard Beeman.
p.   cm.—(Penguin civic classics)
ISBN 978-0-14-312197-8
1. Constitutional history—United States—Sources.   2. United States—Politics
and government—1783–1789.   I. Hamilton, Alexander, 1757–1804.
II. Madison, James, 1751–1836.   III. Jay, John, 1745–1829.
IV. Beeman, Richard R.   V. Title.
KF4515.F4 2012
342.7302'9—dc23   2012023223

Printed in the United States of America
Set in Adobe Caslon
Designed by Sabrina Bowers

CONTENTS

The FEDERALIST PAPERS

We introduce the Penguin Civic Classics series by presenting our readers with a paradox. On the one hand, there is an abundance of evidence establishing that the vast majority of Americans, whatever their political differences, have an intense love of their country, believing that it has been one of the most successful experiments in human freedom and opportunity that the world has ever seen. And Americans are similarly united in having a deep reverence for their Constitution, for their institutions of government, and for the system of free enterprise that has been such a powerful engine for our economic growth. Americans see all of these as playing a vital role in making the nation as successful as it has been.

But there is an equally large body of evidence suggesting that Americans' knowledge of their history and of the way in which their institutions have worked over the course of that history is embarrassingly meager. For example, a third of Americans believe that the Declaration of Independence was written after the end of the Civil War, and fewer than half can identify the three branches of our federal government. Nearly 40 percent of the students at fifty-five of America's elite colleges and universities could not place the Civil War in the correct half century, and fewer than half of them, when presented with the text of the Gettysburg Address, were able to identify it. Nor does it appear that our knowledge improves much as we move closer to the present. Another survey has revealed that more than half of high school seniors thought that Italy, Germany, or Japan was a US ally during the Second World War, and only 14 percent of those seniors could name any relevant fact about US involvement in the Korean War. As the distinguished historian David McCullough has lamented, "While the clamorous popular culture races on, the American past is slipping away, out of sight and out of mind. We are losing our story, forgetting who we are and what it's taken to come this far."

With these discouraging results in front of us, it is no wonder that there is a growing clamor for an increased emphasis on "civic education," defined by one leading authority as "the cultivation of the virtues, knowledge, and skills" necessary for carrying out one's role as a citizen. That very phrase, "civic education," sounds to many like a doctor's prescription: "You need to take your medicine! It may not be very pleasant, but it is something you need to do in order to ensure not only your own health, but also the health of the body politic." It is our hope that reading these volumes in the Penguin Civic Classics series will be much more pleasant than taking medicine, for although these volumes will indeed help improve the reader's civic *knowledge*, we also hope that they will provide some civic *inspiration*—a genuine appreciation for, even an excitement about, some of the words, ideas, and actions that have shaped American society and government since the nation's founding.

The history represented in these volumes, from the founding of the American colonies in the seventeenth century to the adoption of America's Declaration of Independence to Abraham Lincoln's inspiring Gettysburg Address to Barack Obama's inaugural address as the first African American president in American history, is not merely a collection of names and dates to be memorized but, rather, a set of stories to be absorbed and enjoyed. And they are stories that have a real relevance and meaning to our lives today, whether we are debating the nature of America's immigration laws, the extent to which the federal government should be involved in decisions relating to our health care, or, getting even closer to home, whether local schools and school districts have the constitutional right to search a student's locker.

In these volumes, the reader will encounter nearly all of the central themes in American history, as well as the dilemmas and conflicts that have provided much of the dynamism and excitement of that history. The central themes and ideas of American public life—democracy, equality, economic opportunity, the role of government in maintaining that delicate balance between public order and personal freedom, and the government's responsibility to protect certain individual rights—have never remained static, nor have they ever elicited uniform agreement among American citizens.

The very first item in Terry Golway's collection of important American speeches is a sermon given by Massachusetts governor John Winthrop, aboard the ship *Arbella*, as it transported the first Puritan settlers to the new colony. In that sermon, Winthrop described the Puritans' mission in Massachusetts Bay as one of creating a "city upon a hill," a model of virtue and purity for all others in the world to follow. But his vision of that society was in some important respects very much at odds with the values that guide America today. In the opening words of his sermon, Winthrop reminded his fellow colonists that "GOD ALMIGHTY in His most holy and wise providence, hath so disposed of the condition of mankind, as in all times some must be rich, some poor, some high and eminent in power and dignity; others mean and in submission." Hardly a prescription for the democratic society that we claim to be today.

Fast-forward 136 years to the promise contained in Thomas Jefferson's Declaration of Independence that "all men are created equal"—a view of society *very* different from that articulated by Winthrop. Jefferson's city upon a hill was to be a nation dedicated to equality and the pursuit of happiness, not to a divinely ordained, inegalitarian social hierarchy. But, of course, in a world in which Africans were enslaved, women were considered legally subordinate to men, and, indeed, in which many free white males were denied the right to vote because they did not own the requisite amount of property, Jefferson's promise of equality fell far short of an accurate description of the reality of American society in 1776. Still, words have power, and Abraham Lincoln, for one, knew the power of those words. As is amply displayed in Allen Guelzo's volume containing many of Lincoln's principal speeches, time and time again Lincoln invoked Jefferson's preamble as a pledge that Americans of his age were honor-bound to fulfill, describing the preamble as "the electric cord in that Declaration that links the hearts of patriotic and liberty-loving men together, that will link those patriotic hearts as long as the love of freedom exists in the minds of men throughout the world."

Alas, Americans would fight a horrific, bloody civil war in which more than 600,000 people, slave and free, lost their lives before the nation was able to take the steps necessary to forge the link to which Lincoln had referred. Beginning in December 1865, with the adoption of the Thirteenth Amendment, eliminating the institution of slavery; continuing with the adoption of the Fourteenth Amendment (July 1868), with its guarantee of "equal protection under the laws"; and culminating with the adoption of the Fifteenth Amendment (February 1870), asserting that the right to vote could not "be abridged . . . on account of race, color, or previous condition of servitude," those ideas of democracy and equality began to be incorporated into our constitutional system. But although those three amendments represented an important step forward, America's struggle to live up to the promise of the preamble was far from over. It took until 1920 for the nation to adopt the Nineteenth Amendment, giving women the right to vote, and in spite of the guarantees of the Fourteenth and Fifteenth Amendments, the civil rights of African Americans, including the right to vote, continued to be undermined by the actions of individual state governments well into the twentieth century. When Lyndon Johnson, only the second (after Woodrow Wilson) Southern-born president since the Civil War, signed into law the Voting Rights Act of

1965, he too quoted the preamble to the Declaration and ended his speech with a phrase from the anthem of the civil rights movement of the 1950s and 1960s: "We Shall Overcome." And when the first African American president, Barack Obama, delivered his inauguration speech on a cold day in January 2009, he began his speech by paraphrasing the words of Thomas Jefferson's preamble, urging Americans "to carry forward that precious gift, that noble idea, passed on from generation to generation: the God-given promise that all are equal, all are free, and all deserve a chance to pursue their full measure of happiness." Even in 2009 those words were, like Jefferson's, expressions of hope, not descriptions of reality. But they have proved powerful indeed, and they continue to be a dynamic force in shaping the American future just as they have the American past.

Another important theme that emerges from these volumes of Civic Classics involves the age-old debate on how and where to strike the best balance between public order and personal liberty. For most of human history, those who held government power—kings or emperors or czars—usually dealt with that issue by ruthlessly imposing their own definition of what was good for the masses of people whom they governed. When Thomas Paine published his earth-shaking pamphlet *Common Sense* in January 1776, his primary purpose was to persuade the American colonists to throw off British rule, but one of the key elements in his argument was the notion that while every society needs some form of government in order to provide security and protect the freedom of its citizens, the best and freest societies are those in which government is least intrusive. In Paine's words: "Society in every state is a blessing, but government even in its best state is but a necessary evil; in its worst state an intolerable one." Paine's words struck a chord with his American readers, who were already suspicious of the overly powerful, distant government of Great Britain, and the Declaration of Independence, approved seven months later, reinforced that same theme. The distrust of concentrations of government power—the notion that government, while necessary, must be restrained—is deeply rooted in America's revolutionary past, and, of course, is very much alive today, as we can observe by the vitality of political movements such as the Tea Party.

As powerful as Paine's and Jefferson's indictments of excessive British power may have been, they did not provide the answer to the question of how the independent American nation could create a government that would strike an ideal balance between order and liberty. The men who gathered in Philadelphia in the summer of 1787 to frame a new constitution for their still-fragile independent nation took a giant step forward in providing an answer when they created a governmental system based on the division of power between the individual states and the central government—the system that we now call federalism—and by further dividing power among the three branches of the federal government, in a system that we characterize as one of "checks and balances."

But, as in so many other important ideas in American history, those involving federalism and checks and balances were subject to many different interpretations. Alexander Hamilton, James Madison, and John Jay, in the eighty-five essays comprising *The Federalist Papers*, attempted to address some of the concerns that Americans had about the excessive power of the proposed new federal government and, in the process, provided Americans with enduring insights about government and politics—insights that are still cited by Supreme Court justices in their judicial opinions today. But Hamilton and Madison, the two principal authors of *The Federalist Papers*, began to disagree about the relationship of the new federal government to the individual states and to the people at large almost from the moment the new government commenced operation. The debate over the way the words of the Constitution should be interpreted, with Madison and Thomas Jefferson taking a "strict construction" position, and Hamilton, George Washington, and others arguing for a broader interpretation of the Constitution, has stayed with us until the present day. As readers of Jay Feinman's collection of landmark Supreme Court cases will discover, the Court has spent a significant portion of its time over the years, beginning with Chief Justice John Marshall's majority opinion in *McCulloch v. Maryland* (1819), wrestling with the extent of and limits on federal government power. Nor has that conflict been confined to judicial or intellectual arguments. In the years leading up to the Civil War, Northern and Southern politicians fought ferocious battles over the question of what authority the federal government had to legislate with respect to the expansion of slavery into new territories; once again, the ever-eloquent Abraham Lincoln weighed in on those issues, as is amply illustrated in Allen Guelzo's selection of Lincoln speeches. In the end, of course, it was not words that settled the constitutional argument between North and South but the force of arms. The Civil War was, in some senses, America's greatest civic failure, for knowledge and reason alone were not sufficient to settle the conflict between North and South. But however terrible the toll, it did resolve the paradox at the nation's core—the existence of the institution of slavery in a nation that claimed to be devoted to liberty.

Mercifully, the Civil War was the last occasion in which our differences of opinion over governmental power have resulted in warfare, but the war of words has never ceased. Whether debating issues relating to economic regulation, immigration, or providing and regulating health care, Americans—Republicans and Democrats, Tea Party members and Occupy Wall Street activists—continue to differ, sometimes passionately, on the way our Constitution should be interpreted.

Americans, perhaps more than any other people in the world, have been ardently committed to defending their "rights." Indeed, when most Americans today think of their Constitution, they think not so much about those enumerated powers such as the levying of taxes, the regulating of commerce, or the coining of money that are contained in the main body of the Constitution, but, rather, they think of the "Bill of Rights." In fact, one of the few mistakes made by the framers of the Constitution in 1787 was their failure even to include a Bill of Rights in their final draft of the Constitution, a mistake that was, fortunately, remedied by the First Federal Congress in 1789. The rights articulated in our first ten amendments, including freedom of speech, the "free exercise of religion," freedom of the press, and freedom from unlawful search and seizure, have not only provided the foundation for the freedoms that we so value today but also have prompted some of our most vigorously debated controversies. Readers of Jay Feinman's volume on some of the most important Supreme Court decisions in our history will discover that, in general, the court's definition of the rights guaranteed in those amendments has tended to widen over the course of our history. But there remain limits on the Bill of Rights protections enjoyed by Americans. For example, the right of free speech has not extended to public protests in which the threat of violence is imminent, and in an era of GPS tracking devices and CCTV cameras, Americans are confronted with new challenges in defining what constitutes an unlawful search and seizure.

The constitutional protection of individual rights has not been confined to those items specifically enumerated in the Bill of Rights. The Ninth Amendment, which says that the "enumeration in the Constitution, of certain rights, shall not be construed to deny or disparage others retained by the people," has been interpreted to include the right of privacy, including the right of a woman to have some control over her health and reproductive decisions. The best-known of the Supreme Court decisions relating to the right of a woman to terminate a pregnancy, *Roe v. Wade* (1973), far from settling that difficult question, has been followed by a series of subsequent Supreme Court decisions seeking to further refine and, in many cases, limit the right to obtain an abortion. The court's decisions in these areas, far from being legal abstractions of interest only to a few history or civics teachers, have had an impact, and will continue to have an impact, on the lives of millions of women.

This series of Penguin Civic Classics is based on the belief that acquiring knowledge of America's history and of our rights and responsibilities as citizens is not merely an abstract, academic exercise. *It really matters.* It can make a real difference in each and every one of our lives. And never more so than in the extraordinarily complicated, tumultuous, twenty-first-century world in which we live—a time of rapid, sometimes confounding, change. The historian David McCullough has spoken of the way in which our knowledge of history and of the way in which our institutions of government operate can give us a "sense of navigation, a sense of what we've been through in times past and who we are." It can also *empower* us. If we are familiar with the way in which people in the past have confronted their problems, and if we have a decent understanding of how to make the best use of America's institutions to deal with the problems confronting us in the present, we have a much better chance of being able to control our own destinies. Our opinions of the "correct" way to proceed may not always prevail, but we will at least be participants, not passive bystanders, in the ongoing drama that is the history of the United States. And, perhaps most important of all, it is often personally more rewarding, more fun, to be a participant rather than to be a bystander.

RICHARD BEEMAN

On Monday, September 17, 1787, when thirty-nine of the forty-two delegates attending the Constitutional Convention stepped forward to sign a final draft of the document on which they had labored all that summer, the words engrossed on the four parchment sheets sitting on the table before them represented nothing more than *opinion*. At that point the proposed constitution lacked the sanction of the Continental Congress, the official governing body of the "united states." Nor had it achieved the approval of the governments of the thirteen sovereign American states or of "We the people" residing in those states. By the terms of the proposed constitution, the new government of the United States could only take effect after nine of the thirteen states, deliberating in specially called ratifying conventions, added their assent.

Obtaining that assent was not easy. Each of the thirteen states making up the fragile American union under the existing frame of government, the Articles of Confederation, took pride in the independence that they had achieved in the aftermath of an eight-year war with Great Britain. In varying degrees, those states felt some reluctance about yielding any of their authority to a vastly strengthened central government. Moreover, the delegates to the convention in Philadelphia had carried out their proceedings that summer in 1787 in absolute secrecy, so few in the individual states were prepared for the sweeping changes proposed by the new Constitution.

The debate over the Constitution was America's first national referendum—the first time in American history when voters in all of the states were asked to render their opinion on a single subject. And the decision facing Americans as they debated whether or not to approve the proposed Constitution was a stark one: yes or no.

It was an intensely partisan contest. Supporters and opponents of ratification mounted the campaign stump in town and county meetings; local newspapers unleashed a deluge of often-vitriolic equivalents of today's op-eds; and state and local politicians maneuvered behind the scenes to persuade the people of their states to elect either "Federalist" supporters of the Constitution or "Anti-Federalist" opponents to each of the state ratifying conventions. Between late September of 1787 and the fall of 1788, several hundred pamphlets and newspaper essays appeared on the merits and demerits of the Constitution, the largest outpouring of opinion on any subject in the young country's history. Whatever the partisan motives of those pamphlets and essays, the ratification contest produced a body of political writing that sometimes rose above its primary purpose of political persuasion to achieve enduring intellectual importance.

Certainly the best-known of the political writings

to emerge from the debate over the Constitution were the eighty-five essays written by Alexander Hamilton, James Madison, and John Jay, appearing individually under the single pseudonym "Publius," in New York City newspapers between October 1787 and May 1788 and then published together by John and Archibald McLean under the title of *The Federalist*, with the first thirty-six essays appearing on March 22, 1788, and the remaining essays appearing on May 28, 1788.

The man most responsible for conceiving and organizing the effort was in one sense an unlikely choice. Alexander Hamilton, although he was one of the signers of the Constitution, was not wholly pleased with the document. He would have preferred a government based more closely on the aristocratic model of the English Constitution, and his contributions to the debates in the Constitutional Convention were often erratic. But soon after the Convention adjourned, Hamilton seized the initiative in organizing an effort to defend the proposed Constitution against its critics. He first attempted to recruit his friend and political ally Gouverneur Morris to collaborate with him on the essays, but when Morris declined, he turned to his fellow New Yorker John Jay and, later, to James Madison. The choice of Madison—a backup choice, really—would have momentous consequences.

In all, Hamilton wrote fifty-one of the essays; Madison, twenty-nine; and Jay, five (Jay might have made a greater contribution had he not been taken ill after writing four of the first five essays). Although most readers today tend to think of *The Federalist* as a single, coherent body of writing, the essays were written independently under great pressure of time, so there was little opportunity for collaboration among the authors or for them to review or revise their essays. Because of this absence of any coordinated effort, some scholars, aware of the bitter differences that later surfaced between Hamilton and Madison on matters of constitutional interpretation, have commented on the "split personality" of *The Federalist*. But what is most striking from the perspective of the twenty-first century is the remarkable coherence of the essays. Whatever their future disagreements, Madison and Hamilton were able to agree on a division of labor in the writing of the essays that minimized any differences that may have later emerged. In particular, Hamilton may have deliberately muted some of his own desire that the proposed government be even stronger than the one that emerged from the Philadelphia Convention as well as some of his concerns that the new government proposed by the Constitution might be too much influenced by the passions of the people.

Many of the Anti-Federalist opponents of the Constitution feared precisely those things that Hamilton may have privately desired. Although there was no single set of Anti-Federalist writings that matched *The Federalist* in either its immediate impact or in its influence on subsequent generations, Anti-Federalist writers produced an impressive body of work, publishing more than two hundred pamphlets, essays, and broadsides. Because Anti-Federalist critics raised every objection they could possibly devise in their attempt to defeat the Constitution, their critique sometimes lacked the intellectual coherence of *The Federalist*. But the broad themes of their critique—a distrust of concentrations of government power and an emphasis on the role of ordinary citizens in pre-venting government encroachments on the people's liberty—have proved to be of enduring importance in American constitutional and political discourse from that time forward.

The other recurring theme in the Anti-Federalist critique was the absence of a bill of rights in the pro-posed draft of the Constitution as it emerged from the Philadelphia Convention. Try as the Federalists might to argue that a bill of rights was unnecessary, the Anti-Federalists understood that the public at large would not be persuaded by that argument. Indeed, had the Federalists not yielded on that point and promised to add a bill of rights as soon as the new government commenced operation, it is likely that the Constitu-tion would never have gained the approval of the nine states necessary to secure its adoption. Moreover, without the addition of the Bill of Rights, our Consti-tution would have created a union considerably less "perfect" than the "more perfect" one promised in its preamble.

The actual impact of *The Federalist* essays on the out-come of the ratification debate may have been limited. The essays did not circulate much beyond New York until the spring of 1788, so the voters in many states, who elected their delegates prior to that time, were not even familiar with the arguments in them. But over the course of America's history, *The Federalist* essays have reached the status of canonical text of American gov-ernment and constitutionalism. During the period be-tween 1790 and 1800, when leaders of the new republic were engaged in passionate debates over how their new Constitution should be interpreted, *The Fed-*

eralist was cited in Supreme Court opinions only once. In the whole of the nineteenth century, they were cited 58 times. In the first half of the twentieth century Supreme Court justices cited the essays 38 times in their opinions, but in the last half of that century the essays were cited no fewer than 196 times. The trends during the first decade of the twenty-first century suggest that those eighty-five essays are becoming more important as a means by which Americans seek to interpret their Constitution. Some of this increase is almost certainly the consequence of the rising popularity of the doctrines of "originalism" and "original intent," as articulated by Supreme Court justices such as Antonin Scalia and Clarence Thomas; the exceptionally articulate, on occasions brilliant, arguments in favor of the Constitution devised by men such as Hamilton, Madison, and Jay are highly tempting pieces of evidence for those who argue that we should be constrained in our constitutional interpretation by the "original meaning" of that document as it was understood by eighteenth-century Americans at the time the Constitution was drafted and ratified.

But the enduring value of *The Federalist* extends well beyond whatever practical utility the essays may have in settling constitutional disputes in our present day. Although Alexander Hamilton, James Madison, and John Jay conceived of the essays in the context of an eighteenth-century world and in the heat of partisan battle, their insights about law, government, culture, and human nature have a timeless quality. One of the purposes underlying this volume is that Americans, in reading *The Federalist*, will gain a better understanding of the principles underlying our political system and, therefore, a better understanding of our own rights and responsibilities as citizens.

THE SELECTED ESSAYS OF *THE FEDERALIST*

Jacob E. Cooke's complete, modern edition of *The Federalist*, which serves as the textual basis for the essays in this volume, runs to 672 printed pages. Constitutional scholars are likely to differ on precisely which of *The Federalist* essays to include in a volume of selected essays such as this one, but there does seem to be some general agreement about which of the essays have out-lived their immediate, partisan purpose as rejoinders to the Anti-Federalist critique of the Constitution to become more enduring explications of the principles of American constitutionalism.

Of the selections in this volume, eight were written by Alexander Hamilton, ten by James Madison, and one by John Jay. One of the reasons Madison's essays have gained proportionally more attention (given that Madison wrote only slightly more than a third of the essays) than those written by Hamilton is that many of Hamilton's essays, which appeared early in the series, were more partisan in tone, aimed at pointing out the weaknesses of the existing Articles of Confederation and refuting the arguments of his Anti-Federalist opponents. This was an important consideration at the moment the essays were written, but it has seemed of less importance over time. And, as America's constitutional history has unfolded, it has tended to be the Madisonian, rather than the Hamiltonian, view of vitally important issues such as federalism, separation of powers, and checks and balances that has come to dominate modern political thought. Whatever Hamilton's brilliance, it is most often Madison who is referred to as "the father of the Constitution."

Appropriately, though, Hamilton, as the organizer of the enterprise, took the lead in writing most of the early essays. He wrote twenty-seven of the first thirty-six essays, at which point Madison took over, writing twenty-two consecutive essays, from *Federalist* 37 *to Federalist* 58, at which point Hamilton took charge again, writing twenty-four of the remaining twenty-seven essays.

Hamilton's *Federalist* 1 served not only as an introduction to the larger work but also as an appeal to the people to place the broader "public good" ahead of what he described as the "interested or ambitious views" of many of the opponents of the Constitution. This would be a theme in many of Hamilton's essays, and it was often accompanied by an aggressive defense not only of the virtues of an "energetic" government, but also a recitation of the dangers of a weak and divided nation. He would repeat these themes in *Federalist* 6, in which he warned of the threat that "separate confederacies" might pose to the nation at large, and in *Federalist* 15, in which he answered the Anti-Federalists' arguments against a "consolidated" government with a passionate recitation of the ways in which the misdeeds of individual state governments posed a greater threat to the public good than any imagined fears about the excessive power of a national government. He expanded on that theme further in *Federalist* 23, defending not merely the virtues of an "energetic" central government, but also the creation of a standing army—a source of great fear among some Anti-Federalists—in order to provide for the common defense. It is in essays like *Federalist* 15 and 23 that we see Hamilton at his most partisan, vigorously attempting to refute the arguments of his opponents.

James Madison made his entrance as "Publius" with a bang, writing what has become the most famous of all of the *Federalist* essays, number 10, in which he embarked on a distinctly modern approach to the existence of "faction" and "interests" in American politics. Whereas most eighteenth-century commentators believed that the key to good government was to elect virtuous political leaders capable of transcending narrow self-interest, Madison accepted the existence of conflicting interests as an inherent part of any society. Turning prevailing wisdom about politics and government on its head, Madison argued that the best way to control the effects of faction was to extend the sphere of government over a sufficiently large territory so that no one faction could gain undue influence and subvert the public good. Madison continued with this logic in *Federalist* 14, in which he argued that an "extended republic," such as that in America, based as it was on the principle of representation, was in many ways preferable to a direct democracy, such as that of ancient Athens, in which the people themselves "meet and exercise the government in person."

It was in his essays 37 though 58 that Madison really hit his stride. These essays deal with some of the most important issues in American government— republicanism, federalism, separation of powers, and checks and balances. Of these essays, two of the most important are numbers 39, in which Madison describes the proposed new government as being "part national" and "part federal" in character, and number 51, in which he embarks on a brilliant exposition, which he continues in subsequent essays, on the principles of separation of powers and checks and balances.

John Jay recovered from his illness long enough to pen number 64, in which he discusses the treaty-making power of the proposed US Senate—a subject on which Jay was extremely knowledgeable, since he had been one of the principal negotiators of the treaty of peace with England, signed in Paris in September 1783, formally ending the Revolutionary War. Hamilton took over from there. The most important of his concluding essays was number 78, which was probably his most significant contribution to *The Federalist*. Arguing for the importance of protecting "the weakest of the three departments of government," the judiciary, Hamilton defended the provision calling for the appointment of federal judges during a term of "good behavior"; in the process of defending that provision, Hamilton went on to argue that "the interpretation of the laws is the proper and peculiar province of the courts. A constitution is in fact, and must be, regarded by the judges as the fundamental law. It therefore belongs to them to ascertain its meaning as well as the meaning of any law proceeding from the legislative body." The judiciary's power of "judicial review" would not be established as a constitutional precedent until the Supreme Court rendered its decision in *Marbury v. Madison* in 1803, but Hamilton's argument in *Federalist* 78 was an important portent of constitutional developments to come.

The authors of *The Federalist*, along with many of

their counterparts on both sides of the issue of ratification of the Constitution, would not have been so presumptuous as to describe themselves as "political thinkers." But they were, in the best sense of the phrase, "thinking politicians." As historian Gordon Wood has observed, they were writing at a point in history when intellectualism and political activism could naturally coexist. They brought to their work as public officials and political activists an impressive understanding of history and of political philosophy. The essays that emerged from the ratification debate truly have transcended their original, partisan purpose, and, indeed, one can only hope that they might serve as a model for our contemporary politicians and journalists to emulate.

RICHARD BEEMAN

SUGGESTIONS FOR FURTHER READING

The authoritative scholarly edition, on which the excerpts in this volume are modeled, is Jacob E. Cooke, ed., *The Federalist* (Middletown, CT: Wesleyan University Press, 1961). Jack Rakove, *The Federalist: The Essential Essays* (New York: Bedford/St. Martin's Press, 2003) contains a more extensive selection of essays than this volume and is accompanied by a lengthy introduction discussing the intellectual origins of *The Federalist*. Among the dozens of works that have analyzed *The Federalist*, some of the most useful are: David Epstein, *The Political Theory of The Federalist* (Chicago: University of Chicago Press, 1982); Garry Wills, *Explaining America: The Federalist* (Garden City, NY: Doubleday, 1981), and Dan T. Coenen, *The Story of the Federalist: How Hamilton and Madison Reconceived America* (New York: Twelve Tables Press, 2007).

A NOTE
ON THE TEXT

The texts in this edition are based on Jacob E. Cooke's edition of *The Federalist*, published by Wesleyan University Press in 1961; Cooke's edition assembles essays 1 through 77 as they appeared in their first newspaper printing and essays 78 through 85 as they appeared in John and Archibald McLean's second edition of collected essays on May 28, 1788. This volume retains the original lengths of all included essays and follows Cooke's practice of omitting the original titles. Finally, although the title of the McLean edition was simply *The Federalist*, this collection of selected essays follows the modern, common usage in referring to the essays as *The Federalist Papers*.

THE FEDERALIST NO. 1

ALEXANDER HAMILTON

OCTOBER 27, 1787

To the People of the State of New York.

After an unequivocal experience of the inefficacy of the subsisting Fœderal Government, you are called upon to deliberate on a new Constitution for the United States of America. The subject speaks its own importance; comprehending in its consequences, nothing less than the existence of the UNION, the safety and welfare of the parts of which it is composed, the fate of an empire, in many respects, the most interesting in the world. It has been frequently remarked, that it seems to have been reserved to the people of this country, by their conduct and example, to decide the important question, whether societies of men are really capable or not, of establishing good government from reflection and choice, or whether they are forever destined to depend, for their political constitutions, on accident and force. If there be any truth in the remark, the crisis, at which we are arrived, may with propriety be regarded as the æra in which that decision is to be made; and a wrong election of the part we shall act, may, in this view, deserve to be considered as the general misfortune of mankind.

This idea will add the inducements of philanthropy to those of patriotism to heighten the solicitude, which all considerate and good men must feel for the event. Happy will it be if our choice should be directed by a judicious estimate of our true interests, unperplexed and unbiassed by considerations not connected with the public good. But this is a thing more ardently to be wished, than seriously to be expected. The plan offered to our deliberations, affects too many particular interests, innovates upon too many local institutions, not to involve in its discussion a variety of objects foreign to its merits, and of views, passions and prejudices little favourable to the discovery of truth.

Among the most formidable of the obstacles which the new Constitution will have to encounter, may readily be distinguished the obvious interest of a certain class of men in every State to resist all changes which may hazard a diminution of the power, emolument and consequence of the offices they hold under the State-establishments—and the perverted ambition of another class of men, who will either hope to aggrandise themselves by the confusions of their country, or will flatter themselves with fairer prospects of elevation from the subdivision of the empire into several partial confederacies, than from its union under one government.

It is not, however, my design to dwell upon observations of this nature. I am well aware that it would be disingenuous to resolve indiscriminately the opposition of any set of men (merely because their situations might subject them to suspicion) into interested or ambitious views: Candour will oblige us to admit, that even such men may be actuated by upright intentions; and it cannot be doubted that much of the opposition which has made its appearance, or may hereafter make its appearance, will spring from sources, blameless at least, if not respectable, the honest errors of minds led astray by preconceived jealousies and fears. So numerous indeed and so powerful are the causes, which serve to give a false bias to the judgment, that we upon many occasions, see wise and good men on the wrong as well as on the right side of questions, of the first magnitude to society. This circumstance, if duly attended to, would furnish a lesson of moderation to those, who are ever so much persuaded of their being in the right, in any controversy. And a further reason for caution, in this respect, might be drawn from the reflection, that we are not always sure, that those who advocate the truth are influenced by purer principles than their antagonists. Ambition, avarice, personal animosity, party opposition, and many other motives, not more laudable than these, are apt to operate as well upon those who support as upon those who oppose the right side of a question. Were there not even these inducements to moderation, nothing could be more illjudged than that intolerant spirit, which has, at all times, characterised political parties. For, in politics as in religion, it is equally absurd to aim at making proselytes by fire and sword. Heresies in either can rarely be cured by persecution.

And yet however just these sentiments will be allowed to be, we have already sufficient indications, that it will happen in this as in all former cases of great national discussion. A torrent of angry and malignant passions will be let loose. To judge from the conduct of the opposite parties, we shall be led to conclude, that they will mutually hope to evince the justness of their opinions, and to increase the number of their converts by the loudness of their declamations, and by the bitterness of their invectives. An enlightened zeal for the energy and efficiency of government will be stigmatized, as the off-spring of a temper fond of despotic power and hostile to the principles of liberty. An overscrupulous jealousy of danger to the rights of the people, which is more commonly the fault of the head than of the heart, will be represented as mere pretence and artifice; the bait for popularity at the expence of public good. It will be forgotten, on the one hand, that jealousy is the usual concomitant of violent love, and that the noble enthusiasm of liberty is too apt to be infected with a spirit of narrow and illiberal distrust. On the other hand, it will be equally forgotten, that the vigour of government is essential to the security of liberty; that, in the contemplation of a sound and well informed judgment, their interest can never be separated; and that a dangerous ambition more often lurks behind the specious mask of zeal for the rights of the people, than under the forbidding appearance of zeal for the firmness and efficiency of government. History will teach us, that the former has been found a much more certain road to the introduction of despotism, than the latter, and that of those men who have overturned the liberties of republics the greatest number have begun their carreer, by paying an obsequious court to the people, commencing Demagogues and ending Tyrants.

In the course of the preceeding observations I have had an eye, my Fellow Citizens, to putting you upon your guard against all attempts, from whatever quarter, to influence your decision in a matter of the utmost moment to your welfare by any impressions other than those which may result from the evidence of truth. You will, no doubt, at the same time, have collected from the general scope of them that they proceed from a source not unfriendly to the new Constitution. Yes, my Countrymen, I own to you, that, after having given it an attentive consideration, I am clearly of opinion, it is your interest to adopt it. I am convinced, that this is the safest course for your liberty, your dignity, and your happiness. I effect not reserves, which I do not feel. I will not amuse you with an appearance of deliberation, when I have decided. I frankly acknowledge to you my convictions, and I will freely lay before you the reasons on which they are founded. The consciousness of good intentions disdains ambiguity. I shall not however multiply professions on this head. My motives must remain in the depository of my own breast: My arguments will be open to all, and may be judged of by all. They shall at least be offered in a spirit, which will not disgrace the cause of truth.

I propose in a series of papers to discuss the following interesting particulars—*The utility of the* UNION *to your political prosperity—The insufficiency of the present Confederation to preserve that Union—The necessity of a government at least equally energetic with the one proposed to the attainment of this object—The conformity of the proposed constitution to the true principles of republican government—Its analogy to your own state constitution—* and lastly, *The additional security, which its adoption will afford to the preservation of that species of government, to liberty and to property.*

In the progress of this discussion I shall endeavour to give a satisfactory answer to all the objections which shall have made their appearance that may seem to have any claim to your attention.

It may perhaps be thought superfluous to offer arguments to prove the utility of the UNION, a point, no doubt, deeply engraved on the hearts of the great body of the people in every state, and one, which it may be imagined has no adversaries. But the fact is, that we already hear it whispered in the private circles of those who oppose the new constitution, that the Thirteen States are of too great extent for any general system, and that we must of necessity resort to separate confederacies of distinct portions of the whole.* This doctrine will, in all probability, be gradually propagated, till it has votaries enough to countenance an open avowal of it. For nothing can be more evident, to those who are able to take an enlarged view of the subject, than the alternative of an adoption of the new Constitution, or a dismemberment of the Union. It will therefore be of use to begin by examining the advantages of that Union, the certain evils and the probable dangers, to which every State will be exposed from its dissolution. This shall accordingly constitute the subject of my next address.

PUBLIUS.

---

* *The same idea, tracing the arguments to their consequences, is held out in several of the late publications against the New Constitution. (Publius)*

THE FEDERALIST NO. 6

ALEXANDER HAMILTON

NOVEMBER 14, 1787

To the People of the State of New York.

The three last numbers of this Paper have been dedicated to an enumeration of the dangers to which we should be exposed, in a state of disunion, from the arms and arts of foreign nations. I shall now proceed to delineate dangers of a different, and, perhaps, still more alarming kind, those which will in all probability flow from dissentions between the States themselves, and from domestic factions and convulsions. These have been already in some instances slightly anticipated, but they deserve a more particular and more full investigation.

A man must be far gone in Utopian speculations who can seriously doubt, that if these States should either be wholly disunited, or only united in partial confederacies, the subdivisions into which they might be thrown would have frequent and violent contests with each other. To presume a want of motives for such contests, as an argument against their existence, would be to forget that men are ambitious, vindictive and rapacious. To look for a continuation of harmony between a number of independent unconnected sovereignties, situated in the same neighbourhood, would be to disregard the uniform course of human events, and to set at defiance the accumulated experience of ages.

The causes of hostility among nations are innumerable. There are some which have a general and almost constant operation upon the collective bodies of society: Of this description are the love of power or the desire of preeminence and dominion—the jealousy of power, or the desire of equality and safety. There are others which have a more circumscribed, though an equally operative influence, within their spheres: Such are the rivalships and competitions of commerce between commercial nations. And there are others, not less numerous than either of the former, which take their origin intirely in private passions; in the attachments, enmities, interests, hopes and fears of leading individuals in the communities of which they are members. Men of this class, whether the favourites of a king or of a people, have in too many instances abused the confidence they possessed; and assuming the pretext of some public motive, have not scrupled to sacrifice the national tranquility to personal advantage, or personal gratification.

The celebrated Pericles, in compliance with the resentments of a prostitute,* at the expence of much of the blood and treasure of his countrymen, attacked, vanquished and destroyed, the city of the *Samnians*. The same man, stimulated by private pique against the *Megarensians*,† another nation of Greece, or to avoid a prosecution with which he was threatened as an accomplice in a supposed theft of the statuary *Phidias*,‡ or to get rid of the accusations prepared to be brought

---

* *ASPASIA, vide PLUTARCH'S life of Pericles. (Publius)*
† *—Idem. (Publius)*
‡ *—Idem. Phidias was supposed to have stolen some public gold with the connivance of Pericles for the embelishment of the statue of Minerva. (Publius)*

against him for dissipating the funds of the State in the purchase of popularity,* or from a combination of all these causes, was the primitive author of that famous and fatal war, distinguished in the Grecian annals by the name of the *Pelopponesian* war; which, after various vicissitudes, intermissions and renewals, terminated in the ruin of the Athenian commonwealth.

The ambitious Cardinal,|| who was Prime Minister to Henry VIIIth, permitting his vanity to aspire to the Tripple-Crown,† entertained hopes of succeeding in the acquisition of that splendid prize by the influence of the Emperor Charles Vth. To secure the favour and interest of this enterprising and powerful Monarch, he precipitated England into a war with France, contrary to the plainest dictates of Policy, and at the hazard of the safety and independence, as well of the Kingdom over which he presided by his councils, as of Europe in general. For if there ever was a Sovereign who bid fair to realise the project of universal monarchy it was the Emperor Charles Vth, of whose intrigues Wolsey was at once the instrument and the dupe.

The influence which the bigottry of one female,‡ the petulancies of another,§ and the cabals of a third,¶ had in the co[n]temporary policy, ferments and pacifications of a considerable part of Europe are topics that have been too often descanted upon not to be generally known.

To multiply examples of the agency of personal

---

* *Idem. (Publius)*
† *Worn by the Popes. (Publius)*
‡ *Madame De Maintenon. (Publius)*
§ *Dutchess of Marlborough. (Publius)*
¶ *Madame De Pompadoure. (Publius)*

considerations in the production of great national events, either foreign or domestic, according to their direction would be an unnecessary waste of time. Those who have but a superficial acquaintance with the sources from which they are to be drawn will themselves recollect a variety of instances; and those who have a tolerable knowledge of human nature will not stand in need of such lights, to form their opinion either of the reality or extent of that agency. Perhaps however a reference, tending to illustrate the general principle, may with propriety be made to a case which has lately happened among ourselves. If SHAYS had not been a *desperate debtor* it is much to be doubted whether Massachusetts would have been plunged into a civil war.

But notwithstanding the concurring testimony of experience, in this particular, there are still to be found visionary, or designing men, who stand ready to advocate the paradox of perpetual peace between the States, though dismembered and alienated from each other. The genius of republics (say they) is pacific; the spirit of commerce has a tendency to soften the manners of men and to extinguish those inflammable humours which have so often kindled into wars. Commercial republics, like ours, will never be disposed to waste themselves in ruinous contentions with each other. They will be governed by mutual interest, and will cultivate a spirit of mutual amity and concord.

Is it not (we may ask these projectors in politics) the true interest of all nations to cultivate the same benevolent and philosophic spirit? If this be their true interest, have they in fact pursued it? Has it not, on the contrary, invariably been found, that momentary passions and immediate interests have a more active and imperious controul over human conduct than general or remote considerations of policy, utility or justice? Have republics in practice been less addicted to war than monarchies? Are not the former administered by *men* as well as the latter? Are there not aversions, predilections, rivalships and desires of unjust acquisition that affect nations as well as kings? Are not popular assemblies frequently subject to the impulses of rage, resentment, jealousy, avarice, and of other irregular and violent propensities? Is it not well known that their determinations are often governed by a few individuals, in whom they place confidence, and are of course liable to be tinctured by the passions and views of those individuals? Has commerce hitherto done any thing more than change the objects of war? Is not the love of wealth as domineering and enterprising a passion as that of power or glory? Have there not been as many wars founded upon commercial motives, since that has become the prevailing system of nations, as were before occasioned b[y] the cupidity of territory or dominion? Has not the spirit of commerce in many instances administered new incentives to the appetite both for the one and for the other? Let experience the least fallible guide of human opinions be appealed to for an answer to these inquiries.

Sparta, Athens, Rome and Carthage were all Republics; two of them, Athens and Carthage, of the commercial kind. Yet were they as often engaged in wars, offensive and defensive, as the neighbouring Monarchies of the same times. Sparta was little better than a well regulated camp; and Rome was never sated of carnage and conquest.

Carthage, though a commercial Republic, was the aggressor in the very war that ended in her destruction. Hannibal had carried her arms into the heart of Italy and to the gates of Rome, before Scipio, in turn, gave him an overthrow in the territories of Carthage and made a conquest of the Commonwealth.

Venice in latter times figured more than once in wars of ambition; 'till becoming an object of terror to the other Italian States, Pope Julius the Second found means to accomplish that formidable league,* which gave a deadly blow to the power and pride of this haughty Republic.

The Provinces of Holland, 'till they were overwhelmed in debts and taxes, took a leading and conspicuous part in the wars of Europe. They had furious contests with England for the dominion of the sea; and were among the most persevering and most implacable of the opponents of Lewis XIV.

In the government of Britain the representatives of the people compose one branch of the national legislature. Commerce has been for ages the predominant pursuit of that country. Few nations, nevertheless, have been more frequently engaged in war; and the wars, in which that kingdom has been engaged, have in numerous instances proceeded from the people.

There have been, if I may so express it, almost as many popular as royal wars. The cries of the nation and the importunities of their representatives have, upon various occasions, dragged their monarchs into war, or

---

* The LEAGUE OF CAMBRAY, comprehending the Emperor, the King of France, the King of Arragon, and most of the Italian Princes and States. (Publius)

continued them in it contrary to their inclinations, and, sometimes, contrary to the real interests of the State. In that memorable struggle for superiority, between the rival Houses of *Austria* and *Bourbon* which so long kept Europe in a flame, it is well known that the antipathies of the English against the French, seconding the ambition, or rather the avarice of a favourite leader,* protracted the war beyond the limits marked out by sound policy and for a considerable time in opposition to the views of the Court.

The wars of these two last mentioned nations have in a great measure grown out of commercial considerations—The desire of supplanting and the fear of being supplanted either in particular branches of traffic or in the general advantages of trade and navigation; and sometimes even the more culpable desire of sharing in the commerce of other nations, without their consent.

The last war but two between Britain and Spain sprang from the attempts of the English merchants, to prosecute an illicit trade with the Spanish main. These unjustifiable practices on their part produced severities on the part of the Spaniards, towards the subjects of Great Britain, which were not more justifiable; because they exceeded the bounds of a just retaliation, and were chargeable with inhumanity and cruelty. Many of the English who were taken on the Spanish coasts were sent to dig in the mines of Potosi; and by the usual progress of a spirit of resentment, the innocent were after a while confounded with the guilty in indiscriminate punishment. The complaints of the merchants

---

* *The Duke of Marlborough. (Publius)*

kindled a violent flame throughout the nation, which soon after broke out in the house of commons, and was communicated from that body to the ministry. Letters of reprisal were granted and a war ensued, which in its consequences overthrew all the alliances that but twenty years before had been formed, with sanguine expectations of the most beneficial fruits.

From this summary of what has taken place in other countries, whose situations have borne the nearest resemblance to our own, what reason can we have to confide in those reveries, which would seduce us into an expectation of peace and cordiality between the members of the present confederacy, in a state of separation? Have we not already seen enough of the fallacy and extravagance of those idle theories which have amused us with promises of an exemption from the imperfections, weaknesses and evils incident to society in every shape? Is it not time to awake from the deceitful dream of a golden age, and to adopt as a practical maxim for the direction of our political conduct, that we, as well as the other inhabitants of the globe, are yet remote from the happy empire of perfect wisdom and perfect virtue?

Let the point of extreme depression to which our national dignity and credit have sunk—let the inconveniences felt every where from a lax and ill administration of government—let the revolt of a part of the State of North-Carolina—the late menacing disturbances in Pennsylvania and the actual insurrections and rebellions in Massachusetts declare.

So far is the general sense of mankind from corresponding with the tenets of those, who endeavour to lull asleep our apprehensions of discord and hostility between the States, in the event of disunion, that it has from long observation of the progress of society become a sort of axiom in politics, that vicinity, or nearness of situation, constitutes nations natural enemies. An intelligent writer expresses himself on this subject to this effect—"NEIGHBOURING NATIONS (says he) are naturally ENEMIES of each other, unless their common weakness forces them to league in a CONFEDERATE REPUBLIC, and their constitution prevents the differences that neighbourhood occasions, extinguishing that secret jealousy, which disposes all States to aggrandise themselves at the expence of their neighbours."* This passage, at the same time points out the evil and suggests the REMEDY.

PUBLIUS.

THE FEDERALIST NO. 9

ALEXANDER HAMILTON

NOVEMBER 21, 1787

To the People of the State of New York.

A Firm Union will be of the utmost moment to the peace and liberty of the States as a barrier against domestic faction and insurrection. It is impossible to read the history of the petty Republics of Greece and Italy, without feeling sensations of horror and disgust at the distractions with which they were continually agitated,

---

* *Vide Principes des Negotiations par L'Abbe de Mably. (Publius)*

and at the rapid succession of revolutions, by which they were kept in a state of perpetual vibration, between the extremes of tyranny and anarchy. If they exhibit occasional calms, these only serve as short-lived contrasts to the furious storms that are to succeed. If now and then intervals of felicity open themselves to view, we behold them with a mixture of regret arising from the reflection that the pleasing scenes before us are soon to be overwhelmed by the tempestuous waves of sedition and party-rage. If momentary rays of glory break forth from the gloom, while they dazzle us with a transient and fleeting brilliancy, they at the same time admonish us to lament that the vices of government should pervert the direction and tarnish the lustre of those bright talents and exalted indowments, for which the favoured soils, that produced them, have been so justly celebrated.

From the disorders that disfigure the annals of those republics, the advocates of despotism have drawn arguments, not only against the forms of republican government, but against the very principles of civil liberty. They have decried all free government, as inconsistent with the order of society, and have indulged themselves in malicious exultation over its friends and partizans. Happily for mankind, stupendous fabrics reared on the basis of liberty, which have flourished for ages, have in a few glorious instances refuted their gloomy sophisms. And, I trust, America will be the broad and solid foundation of other edifices not less magnificent, which will be equally permanent monuments of their errors.

But it is not to be denied that the portraits, they have sketched of republican government, were too just copies of the originals from which they were taken. If it had been found impracticable, to have devised models of a more perfect structure, the enlightened friends to liberty would have been obliged to abandon the cause of that species of government as indefensible. The science of politics, however, like most other sciences has received great improvement. The efficacy of various principles is now well understood, which were either not known at all, or imperfectly known to the ancients. The regular distribution of power into distinct departments—the introduction of legislative ballances and checks—the institution of courts composed of judges, holding their offices during good behaviour—the representation of the people in the legislature by deputies of their own election—these are either wholly new discoveries or have made their principal progress towards perfection in modern times. They are means, and powerful means, by which the excellencies of republican government may be retained and its imperfections lessened or avoided. To this catalogue of circumstances, that tend to the amelioration of popular systems of civil government, I shall venture, however novel it may appear to some, to add one more on a principle, which has been made the foundation of an objection to the New Constitution, I mean the EN-LARGEMENT of the ORBIT within which such systems are to revolve either in respect to the dimensions of a single State, or to the consolidation of several smaller States into one great confederacy. The latter is that which immediately concerns the object under consideration. It will however be of use to examine the principle in its application to a single State which shall be attended to in another place.

The utility of a confederacy, as well to suppress faction and to guard the internal tranquillity of States, as to increase their external force and security, is in reality not a new idea. It has been practiced upon in different countries and ages, and has received the sanction of the most applauded writers, on the subjects of politics. The opponents of the PLAN proposed have with great assiduity cited and circulated the observations of Montesquieu on the necessity of a contracted territory for a republican government. But they seem not to have been apprised of the sentiments of that great man expressed in another part of his work, nor to have adverted to the consequences of the principle to which they subscribe, with such ready acquiescence.

When Montesquieu recommends a small extent for republics, the standards he had in view were of dimensions, far short of the limits of almost every one of these States. Neither Virginia, Massachusetts, Pennsylvania, New-York, North-Carolina, nor Georgia, can by any means be compared with the models, from which he reasoned and to which the terms of his description apply. If we therefore take his ideas on this point, as the criterion of truth, we shall be driven to the alternative, either of taking refuge at once in the arms of monarchy, or of spliting ourselves into an infinity of little jealous, clashing, tumultuous commonwealths, the wretched nurseries of unceasing discord and the miserable objects of universal pity or contempt. Some of the writers, who have come forward on the other side of the question, seem to have been aware of the dilemma; and have even been bold enough to hint at the division of the larger States, as a desirable thing. Such an infatuated policy, such a desperate expedient, might, by the multiplication of petty offices, answer the views of men, who possess not qualifications to extend their influence beyond the narrow circles of personal intrigue, but it could never promote the greatness or happiness of the people of America.

Referring the examination of the principle itself to another place, as has been already mentioned, it will be sufficient to remark here, that in the sense of the author who has been most emphatically quoted upon the occasion, it would only dictate a reduction of the SIZE of the more considerable MEMBERS of the Union; but would not militate against their being all comprehended in one Confederate Government. And this is the true question, in the discussion of which we are at present interested.

So far are the suggestions of Montesquieu from standing in opposition to a general Union of the States, that he explicitly treats of a CONFEDERATE REPUBLIC as the expedient for extending the sphere of popular government and reconciling the advantages of monarchy with those of republicanism.

"It is very probable (says he*) that mankind would have been obliged, at length, to live constantly under the government of a SINGLE PERSON, had they not contrived a kind of constitution, that has all the internal advantages of a republican, together with the external force of a monarchial government. I mean a CONFEDERATE REPUBLIC.

"This form of Government is a Convention, by which several smaller *States* agree to become members of a larger *one*, which they intend to form. It is a kind

---

* *Spirit of Laws, Vol. I. Book IX. Chap. I. (Publius)*

of assemblage of societies, that constitute a new one, capable of encreasing by means of new associations, till they arrive to such a degree of power as to be able to provide for the security of the united body.

"A republic of this kind, able to withstand an external force, may support itself without any internal corruption. The form of this society prevents all manner of inconveniencies.

"If a single member should attempt to usurp the supreme authority, he could not be supposed to have an equal authority and credit, in all the confederate states. Were he to have too great influence over one, this would alarm the rest. Were he to subdue a part, that which would still remain free might oppose him with forces, independent of those which he had usurped, and overpower him before he could be settled in his usurpation.

"Should a popular insurrection happen, in one of the confederate States, the others are able to quell it. Should abuses creep into one part, they are reformed by those that remain sound. The State may be destroyed on one side, and not on the other; the confederacy may be dissolved, and the confederates preserve their sovereignty.

"As this government is composed of small republics it enjoys the internal happiness of each, and with respect to its external situation it is possessed, by means of the association of all the advantages of large monarchies."

I have thought it proper to quote at length these interesting passages, because they contain a luminous abrigement of the principal arguments in favour of the Union, and must effectually remove the false impressions, which a misapplication of other parts of the work was calculated to produce. They have at the same time an intimate connection with the more immediate design of this Paper; which is to illustrate the tendency of the Union to repress domestic faction and insurrection.

A distinction, more subtle than accurate has been raised between a *confederacy* and a *consolidation* of the States. The essential characteristic of the first is said to be, the restriction of its authority to the members in their collective capacities, without reaching to the individuals of whom they are composed. It is contended that the national council ought to have no concern with any object of internal administration. An exact equality of suffrage between the members has also been insisted upon as a leading feature of a Confederate Government. These positions are in the main arbitary; they are supported neither by principle nor precedent. It has indeed happened that governments of this kind have generally operated in the manner, which the distinction, taken notice of, supposes to be inherent in their nature—but there have been in most of them extensive exceptions to the practice, which serve to prove as far as example will go, that there is no absolute rule on the subject. And it will be clearly shewn, in the course of this investigation, that as far as the principle contended for has prevailed, it has been the cause of incurable disorder and imbecility in the government.

The definition of a *Confederate Republic* seems simply to be, an "assemblage of societies" or an association of two or more States into one State. The extent, modifications and objects of the Fœderal authority are mere matters of discretion. So long as the separate organisation of the members be not abolished, so long as it exists by a constitutional necessity for local purposes, though it should be in perfect subordination to the general authority of the Union, it would still be, in fact and in theory, an association of States, or a confederacy. The proposed Constitution, so far from implying an abolition of the State Governments, makes them constituent parts of the national sovereignty by allowing them a direct representation in the Senate, and leaves in their possession certain exclusive and very important portions of sovereign power. This fully corresponds, in every rational import of the terms, with the idea of a Fœderal Government.

In the Lycian confederacy, which consisted of twenty three CITIES or republics, the largest were entitled to *three* votes in the COMMON COUNCIL, those of the middle class to *two* and the smallest to *one*. The COMMON COUNCIL had the appointment of all the judges and magistrates of the respective CITIES. This was certainly the most delicate species of interference in their internal administration; for if there be any thing, that seems exclusively appropriated to the local jurisdictions, it is the appointment of their own officers. Yet Montesquieu, speaking of this association, says "Were I to give a model of an excellent confederate republic, it would be that of Lycia." Thus we perceive that the distinctions insisted upon were not within the contemplation of this enlightened civilian, and we shall be led to conclude that they are the novel refinements of an erroneous theory.

PUBLIUS.

THE FEDERALIST NO. 10

JAMES MADISON

NOVEMBER 22, 1787

To the People of the State of New York.

Among the numerous advantages promised by a well constructed Union, none deserves to be more accurately developed than its tendency to break and control the violence of faction. The friend of popular governments, never finds himself so much alarmed for their character and fate, as when he contemplates their propensity to this dangerous vice. He will not fail therefore to set a due value on any plan which, without violating the principles to which he is attached, provides a proper cure for it. The instability, injustice and confusion introduced into the public councils, have in truth been the mortal diseases under which popular governments have every where perished; as they continue to be the favorite and fruitful topics from which the adversaries to liberty derive their most specious declamations. The valuable improvements made by the American Constitutions on the popular models, both ancient and modern, cannot certainly be too much admired; but it would be an unwarrantable partiality, to contend that they have as effectually obviated the danger on this side as was wished and expected. Complaints are every where heard from our most considerate and virtuous citizens, equally the friends of public and private faith, and of public and personal liberty; that our governments are too unstable; that the public good is disregarded in the conflicts of rival parties; and that measures are too often decided, not according to the rules of justice, and the rights of the minor party; but by the superior force of an interested and over-bearing majority. However anxiously we may wish that these complaints had no foundation, the evidence of known facts will not permit us to deny that they are in some degree true. It will be found indeed, on a candid review of our situation, that some of the distresses under which we labor, have been erroneously charged on the operation of our governments; but it will be found, at the same time, that other causes will not alone account for many of our heaviest misfortunes; and particularly, for that prevailing and increasing distrust of public engagements, and alarm for private rights, which are echoed from one end of the continent to the other. These must be chiefly, if not wholly, effects of the unsteadiness and injustice, with which a factious spirit has tainted our public administrations.

By a faction I understand a number of citizens, whether amounting to a majority or minority of the whole, who are united and actuated by some common impulse of passion, or of interest, adverse to the rights of other citizens, or to the permanent and aggregate interests of the community.

There are two methods of curing the mischiefs of faction: the one, by removing its causes; the other, by controlling its effects.

There are again two methods of removing the causes of faction: the one by destroying the liberty which is essential to its existence; the other, by giving to every citizen the same opinions, the same passions, and the same interests.

It could never be more truly said than of the first remedy, that it is worse than the disease. Liberty is to faction, what air is to fire, an aliment without which it instantly expires. But it could not be a less folly to abolish liberty, which is essential to political life, because it nourishes faction, than it would be to wish the annihilation of air, which is essential to animal life, because it imparts to fire its destructive agency.

The second expedient is as impracticable, as the first would be unwise. As long as the reason of man continues fallible, and he is at liberty to exercise it, different opinions will be formed. As long as the connection subsists between his reason and his self-love, his opinions and his passions will have a reciprocal influence on each other; and the former will be objects to which the latter will attach themselves. The diversity in the faculties of men from which the rights of property originate, is not less an insuperable obstacle to a uniformity of interests. The protection of these faculties is the first object of Government. From the protection of different and unequal faculties of acquiring property, the possession of different degrees and kinds of property immediately results: and from the influence of these on the sentiments and views of the respective proprietors, ensues a division of the society into different interests and parties.

The latent causes of faction are thus sown in the nature of man; and we see them every where brought into different degrees of activity, according to the different circumstances of civil society. A zeal for different opinions concerning religion, concerning Government and many other points, as well of speculation as of practice; an attachment to different leaders ambitiously contending for pre-eminence and power; or to persons of other descriptions whose fortunes have been interesting to the human passions, have in turn divided mankind into parties, inflamed them with mutual animosity, and rendered them much more disposed to vex and oppress each other, than to co-operate for their common good. So strong is this propensity of mankind to fall into mutual animosities, that where no substantial occasion presents itself, the most frivolous and fanciful distinctions have been sufficient to kindle their unfriendly passions, and excite their most violent conflicts. But the most common and durable source of factions, has been the various and unequal distribution of property. Those who hold, and those who are without property, have ever formed distinct interests in society. Those who are creditors, and those who are debtors, fall under a like discrimination. A landed interest, a manufacturing interest, a mercantile interest, a monied interest, with many lesser interests, grow up of necessity in civilized nations, and divide them into different classes, actuated by different sentiments and views. The regulation of these various and interfering interests forms the principal task of modern Legislation, and involves the spirit of party and faction in the necessary and ordinary operations of Government.

No man is allowed to be a judge in his own cause; because his interest would certainly bias his judgment, and, not improbably, corrupt his integrity. With equal, nay with greater reason, a body of men, are unfit to be both judges and parties, at the same time; yet, what are many of the most important acts of legislation, but so many judicial determinations, not indeed concerning the rights of single persons, but concerning the rights of large bodies of citizens; and what are the different classes of legislators, but advocates and parties to the causes which they determine? Is a law proposed concerning private debts? It is a question to which the creditors are parties on one side, and the debtors on the other. Justice ought to hold the balance between them. Yet the parties are and must be themselves the judges; and the most numerous party, or, in other words, the most powerful faction must be expected to prevail. Shall domestic manufactures be encouraged, and in what degree, by restrictions on foreign manufactures? are questions which would be differently decided by the landed and the manufacturing classes; and probably by neither, with a sole regard to justice and the public good. The apportionment of taxes on the various descriptions of property, is an act which seems to require the most exact impartiality; yet, there is perhaps no legislative act in which greater opportunity and temptation are given to a predominant party, to trample on the rules of justice. Every shilling with which they over-burden the inferior number, is a shilling saved to their own pockets.

It is in vain to say, that enlightened statesmen will be able to adjust these clashing interests, and render them all subservient to the public good. Enlightened statesmen will not always be at the helm: Nor, in many cases, can such an adjustment be made at all, without taking into view indirect and remote considerations, which will rarely prevail over the immediate interest which one party may find in disregarding the rights of another, or the good of the whole.

The inference to which we are brought, is, that the *causes* of faction cannot be removed; and that relief is only to be sought in the means of controlling its *effects*.

If a faction consists of less than a majority, relief is supplied by the republican principle, which enables the majority to defeat its sinister views by regular vote: It may clog the administration, it may convulse the society; but it will be unable to execute and mask its violence under the forms of the Constitution. When a majority is included in a faction, the form of popular government on the other hand enables it to sacrifice to its ruling passion or interest, both the public good and the rights of other citizens. To secure the public good, and private rights, against the danger of such a faction, and at the same time to preserve the spirit and the form of popular government, is then the great object to which our enquiries are directed: Let me add that it is the great desideratum, by which alone this form of government can be rescued from the opprobrium under which it has so long labored, and be recommended to the esteem and adoption of mankind.

By what means is this object attainable? Evidently by one of two only. Either the existence of the same passion or interest in a majority at the same time, must be prevented; or the majority, having such co-existent passion or interest, must be rendered, by their number and local situation, unable to concert and carry into effect schemes of oppression. If the impulse and the opportunity be suffered to coincide, we well know that neither moral nor religious motives can be relied on as an adequate control. They are not found to be such on the injustice and violence of individuals, and lose their efficacy in proportion to the number combined together; that is, in proportion as their efficacy becomes needful.

From this view of the subject, it may be concluded, that a pure Democracy, by which I mean, a Society, consisting of a small number of citizens, who assemble and administer the Government in person, can admit of no cure for the mischiefs of faction. A common passion or interest will, in almost every case, be felt by a majority of the whole; a communication and concert results from the form of Government itself; and there is nothing to check the inducements to sacrifice the weaker party, or an obnoxious individual. Hence it is, that such Democracies have ever been spectacles of turbulence and contention; have ever been found incompatible with personal security, or the rights of property; and have in general been as short in their lives, as they have been violent in their deaths. Theoretic politicians, who have patronized this species of Government, have erroneously supposed, that by reducing mankind to a perfect equality in their political rights, they would, at the same time, be perfectly equalized and assimilated in their possessions, their opinions, and their passions.

A Republic, by which I mean a Government in which the scheme of representation takes place, opens a different prospect, and promises the cure for which we are seeking. Let us examine the points in which it varies from pure Democracy, and we shall comprehend both the nature of the cure, and the efficacy which it must derive from the Union.

The two great points of difference between a Democracy and a Republic are, first, the delegation of the Government, in the latter, to a small number of citizens elected by the rest: secondly, the greater number of citizens, and greater sphere of country, over which the latter may be extended.

The effect of the first difference is, on the one hand to refine and enlarge the public views, by passing them through the medium of a chosen body of citizens, whose wisdom may best discern the true interest of their country, and whose patriotism and love of justice, will be least likely to sacrifice it to temporary or partial considerations. Under such a regulation, it may well happen that the public voice pronounced by the representatives of the people, will be more consonant to the public good, than if pronounced by the people themselves convened for the purpose. On the other hand, the effect may be inverted. Men of factious tempers, of local prejudices, or of sinister designs, may by intrigue, by corruption or by other means, first obtain the suffrages, and then betray the interests of the people. The question resulting is, whether small or extensive Republics are most favorable to the election of proper guardians of the public weal: and it is clearly decided in favor of the latter by two obvious considerations.

In the first place it is to be remarked that however small the Republic may be, the Representatives must be raised to a certain number, in order to guard against the cabals of a few; and that however large it may be, they must be limited to a certain number, in order to guard against the confusion of a multitude. Hence the number of Representatives in the two cases, not being in proportion to that of the Constituents, and being proportionally greatest in the small Republic, it follows, that if the proportion of fit characters, be not less, in the large than in the small Republic, the former will present a greater option, and consequently a greater probability of a fit choice.

In the next place, as each Representative will be chosen by a greater number of citizens in the large than in the small Republic, it will be more difficult for unworthy candidates to practise with success the vicious arts, by which elections are too often carried; and the suffrages of the people being more free, will be more likely to centre on men who possess the most attractive merit, and the most diffusive and established characters.

It must be confessed, that in this, as in most other cases, there is a mean, on both sides of which inconveniencies will be found to lie. By enlarging too much the number of electors, you render the representative too little acquainted with all their local circumstances and lesser interests; as by reducing it too much, you render him unduly attached to these, and too little fit to comprehend and pursue great and national objects. The Federal Constitution forms a happy combination in this respect; the great and aggregate interests being referred to the national, the local and particular, to the state legislatures.

The other point of difference is, the greater number of citizens and extent of territory which may be brought within the compass of Republican, than of Democratic Government; and it is this circumstance principally which renders factious combinations less to be dreaded in the former, than in the latter. The smaller the society, the fewer probably will be the distinct parties and interests composing it; the fewer the distinct parties and interests, the more frequently will a majority be found of the same party; and the smaller the number of individuals composing a majority, and the smaller the compass within which they are placed, the more easily will they concert and execute their plans of oppression. Extend the sphere, and you take in a greater variety of parties and interests; you make it less probable that a majority of the whole will have a common motive to invade the rights of other citizens; or if such a common motive exists, it will be more difficult for all who feel it to discover their own strength, and to act in unison with each other. Besides other impediments, it may be remarked, that where there is a consciousness of unjust or dishonorable purposes, communication is always checked by distrust, in proportion to the number whose concurrence is necessary.

Hence it clearly appears, that the same advantage, which a Republic has over a Democracy, in controlling the effects of faction, is enjoyed by a large over a small Republic—is enjoyed by the Union over the States composing it. Does this advantage consist in the substitution of Representatives, whose enlightened views and virtuous sentiments render them superior to local prejudices, and to schemes of injustice? It will not be denied, that the Representation of the Union will be most likely to possess these requisite endowments. Does it consist in the greater security afforded by a greater variety of parties, against the event of any one party being able to outnumber and oppress the rest? In an equal degree does the encreased variety of parties, comprised within the Union, encrease this security. Does it, in fine, consist in the greater obstacles opposed to the concert and accomplishment of the secret wishes of an unjust and interested majority?

Here, again, the extent of the Union gives it the most palpable advantage.

The influence of factious leaders may kindle a flame within their particular States, but will be unable to spread a general conflagration through the other States: a religious sect, may degenerate into a political faction in a part of the Confederacy but the variety of sects dispersed over the entire face of it must secure the national Councils against any danger from that source: a rage for paper money, for an abolition of debts, for an equal division of property, or for any other improper or wicked project, will be less apt to pervade the whole body of the Union, than a particular member of it; in the same proportion as such a malady is more likely to taint a particular county or district, than an entire State.

In the extent and proper structure of the Union, therefore we behold a Republican remedy for the diseases most incident to Republican Government. And according to the degree of pleasure and pride, we feel in being Republicans, ought to be our zeal cherishing the spirit, and supporting the character of Federalists.

PUBLIUS.

JAMES MADISON

NOVEMBER 30, 1787

To the People of the State of New York.

We have seen the necessity of the union as our bulwark against foreign danger, as the conservator of peace among ourselves, as the guardian of our commerce and other common interests, as the only substitute for those military establishments which have subverted the liberties of the old world; and as the proper antidote for the diseases of faction, which have proved fatal to other popular governments, and of which alarming symptoms have been betrayed by our own. All that remains, within this branch of our enquiries, is to take notice of an objection, that may be drawn from the great extent of country which the union embraces. A few observations on this subject will be the more proper, as it is perceived that the adversaries of the new constitution are availing themselves of a prevailing prejudice, with regard to the practicable sphere of republican administration, in order to supply by imaginary difficulties, the want of those solid objections, which they endeavor in vain to find.

The error which limits Republican Government to a narrow district, has been unfolded and refuted in preceding papers. I remark here only, that it seems to owe its rise and prevalence, chiefly to the confounding of a republic with a democracy: And applying to the former reasonings drawn from the nature of the latter.

The true distinction between these forms was also adverted to on a former occasion. It is, that in a democracy, the people meet and exercise the government in person; in a republic they assemble and administer it by their representatives and agents. A democracy consequently will be confined to a small spot. A republic may be extended over a large region.

To this accidental source of the error may be added the artifice of some celebrated authors, whose writings have had a great share in forming the modern standard of political opinions. Being subjects either of an absolute, or limited monarchy, they have endeavored to heighten the advantages or palliate the evils of those forms; by placing in comparison with them, the vices and defects of the republican, and by citing as specimens of the latter, the turbulent democracies of ancient Greece, and modern Italy. Under the confusion of names, it has been an easy task to transfer to a republic, observations applicable to a democracy only, and among others, the observation that it can never be established but among a small number of people, living within a small compass of territory.

Such a fallacy may have been the less perceived as most of the governments of antiquity were of the democratic species; and even in modern Europe, to which we owe the great principle of representation, no example is seen of a government wholly popular, and founded at the same time wholly on that principle. If Europe has the merit of discovering this great mechanical power in government, by the simple agency of which, the will of the largest political body may be concentred, and its force directed to any object, which the public good requires; America can claim the merit of making the discovery the basis of unmixed and extensive republics. It is only to be lamented, that any of her citizens should wish to deprive her of the additional merit of displaying its full efficacy on the establishment of the comprehensive system now under her consideration.

As the natural limit of a democracy is that distance from the central point, which will just permit the most remote citizens to assemble as often as their public functions demand; and will include no greater number than can join in those functions; so the natural limit of a republic is that distance from the center, which will barely allow the representatives of the people to meet as often as may be necessary for the administration of public affairs. Can it be said, that the limits of the United States exceed this distance? It will not be said by those who recollect that the Atlantic coast is the longest side of the union; that during the term of thirteen years, the representatives of the States have been almost continually assembled; and that the members from the most distant States are not chargeable with greater intermissions of attendance, than those from the States in the neighbourhood of Congress.

That we may form a juster estimate with regard to this interesting subject, let us resort to the actual dimensions of the union. The limits as fixed by the treaty of peace are on the east the Atlantic, on the south the latitude of thirty-one degrees, on the west the Mississippi, and on the north an irregular line running in some instances beyond the forty-fifth degree, in others falling as low as the forty-second. The southern shore of Lake Erie lies below that latitude. Computing the distance between the thirty-one and forty-five degrees, it amounts to nine hundred and seventy-three common miles; computing it from thirty-one to forty-two degrees to seven hundred, sixty four miles and an half. Taking the mean for the distance, the amount will be eight hundred, sixty-eight miles and three-fourths. The mean distance from the Atlantic to the Mississippi does not probably exceed seven hundred and fifty miles. On a comparison of this extent, with that of several countries in Europe, the practicability of rendering our system commensurate to it, appears to be demonstrable. It is not a great deal larger than Germany, where a Diet representing the whole empire is continually assembled; or than Poland before the late dismemberment, where another national Diet was the depository of the supreme power. Passing by France and Spain, we find that in Great Britain, inferior as it may be in size, the representatives of the northern extremity of the island, have as far to travel to the national Council, as will be required of those of the most remote parts of the union.

Favorable as this view of the subject may be, some observations remain which will place it in a light still more satisfactory.

In the first place it is to be remembered, that the general government is not to be charged with the whole power of making and administering laws. Its jurisdiction is limited to certain enumerated objects, which concern all the members of the republic, but which are not to be attained by the separate provisions of any. The subordinate governments which can extend their care to all those other objects, which can be separately provided for, will retain their due authority and activity. Were it proposed by the plan of the Convention to abolish the governments of the particular States, its adversaries would have some ground for their objection, though it would not be difficult to shew that if they were abolished, the general government would be compelled by the principle of self-preservation, to reinstate them in their proper jurisdiction.

A second observation to be made is, that the immediate object of the Fœderal Constitution is to secure the union of the Thirteen Primitive States, which we know to be practicable; and to add to them such other States, as may arise in their own bosoms or in their neighbourhoods, which we cannot doubt to be equally practicable. The arrangements that may be necessary for those angles and fractions of our territory, which lie on our north western frontier, must be left to those whom further discoveries and experience will render more equal to the task.

Let it be remarked in the third place, that the intercourse throughout the union will be daily facilitated by new improvements. Roads will every where be shortened, and kept in better order; accommodations for travellers will be multiplied and meliorated; and interior navigation on our eastern side will be opened throughout, or nearly throughout the whole extent of the Thirteen States. The communication between the western and Atlantic districts, and between different parts of each, will be rendered more and more easy by those numerous canals with which the beneficence of nature has intersected our country, and which art finds it so little difficult to connect and complete.

A fourth and still more important consideration is, that as almost every State will on one side or other, be a frontier, and will thus find in a regard to its safety, an inducement to make some sacrifices for the sake of the general protection; so the States which lie at the greatest distance from the heart of the union, and which of course may partake least of the ordinary circulation of its benefits, will be at the same time immediately contiguous to foreign nations, and will consequently stand on particular occasions, in greatest need of its strength and resources. It may be inconvenient for Georgia or the States forming our western or north eastern borders to send their representatives to the seat of government, but they would find it more so to struggle alone against an invading enemy, or even to support alone the whole expence of those precautions, which may be dictated by the neighbourhood of continual danger. If they should derive less benefit therefore from the union in some respects, than the less distant States, they will derive greater benefit from it in other respects, and thus the proper equilibrium will be maintained throughout.

I submit to you my fellow citizens, these considerations, in full confidence that the good sense which has so often marked your decisions, will allow them their due weight and effect; and that you will never suffer difficulties, however formidable in appearance or however fashionable the error on which they may be founded, to drive you into the gloomy and perilous scene into which the advocates for disunion would conduct you. Hearken not to the unnatural voice which tells you that the people of America, knit together as they are by so many chords of affection, can no longer live together as members of the same family; can no longer continue the mutual guardians of their mutual happiness; can no longer be fellow citizens of one great respectable and flourishing empire. Hearken not to the voice which petulantly tells you that the form of government recommended for your adoption is a novelty in the political world; that it has never yet had a place in the theories of the wildest projectors; that it rashly attempts what it is impossible to accomplish. No my countrymen, shut your ears against this unhallowed language. Shut your hearts against the poison which it conveys; the kindred blood which flows in the veins of American citizens, the mingled blood which they have shed in defence of their sacred rights, consecrate their union, and excite horror at the idea of their becoming aliens, rivals, enemies. And if novelties are to be shunned, believe me the most alarming of all novelties, the most wild of all projects, the most rash of all attempts, is that of rending us in pieces, in order to preserve our liberties and promote our happiness. But why is the experiment of an extended republic to be rejected merely because it may comprise what is new? Is it not the glory of the people of America, that whilst they have paid a decent regard to the opinions of former times and other nations, they have not suffered a blind veneration for antiquity, for custom, or for names, to overrule the suggestions of their own good sense, the knowledge of their own situation, and the lessons of their own experience? To this manly spirit, posterity will be indebted for the possession, and the world for the example of the numerous innovations displayed on the American theatre, in favor of private rights and public happiness. Had no important step been taken by the leaders of the revolution for which a precedent could not be discovered, no government established of which an exact model did not present itself, the people of the United States might, at this moment, have been numbered among the melancholy victims of misguided councils, must at best have been labouring under the weight of some of those forms which have crushed the liberties of the rest of mankind. Happily for America, happily we trust for the whole human race, they pursued a new and more noble course. They accomplished a revolution which has no parallel in the annals of human society: They reared the fabrics of governments which have no model on the face of the globe. They formed the design of a great confederacy, which it is incumbent on their successors to improve and perpetuate. If their works betray imperfections, we wonder at the fewness of them. If they erred most in the structure of the union; this was the work most difficult to be executed; this is the work which has been new modelled by the act of your Convention, and it is that act on which you are now to deliberate and to decide.

PUBLIUS.

THE FEDERALIST NO. 23

ALEXANDER HAMILTON

DECEMBER 18, 1787

To the People of the State of New York.

The necessity of a Constitution, at least equally energetic with the one proposed, to the preservation of the Union, is the point, at the examination of which we are now arrived.

This enquiry will naturally divide itself into three branches—the objects to be provided for by a Fœderal Government—the quantity of power necessary to the accomplishment of those objects—the persons upon whom that power ought to operate. Its distribution and organization will more properly claim our attention under the succeeding head.

The principal purposes to be answered by Union are these—The common defence of the members—the preservation of the public peace as well against internal convulsions as external attacks—the regulation of commerce with other nations and between the States— the superintendence of our intercourse, political and commercial, with foreign countries.

The authorities essential to the care of the common defence are these—to raise armies—to build and equip fleets—to prescribe rules for the government of both— to direct their operations—to provide for their support. These powers ought to exist without limitation: *Because it is impossible to foresee or define the extent and variety of national exigencies, or the correspondent extent & variety of the means which may be necessary to satisfy them.* The circumstances that endanger the safety of nations are infinite; and for this reason no constitutional shackles can wisely be imposed on the power to which the care of it is committed. This power ought to be co-extensive with all the possible combinations of such circumstances; and ought to be under the direction of the same councils, which are appointed to preside over the common defence.

This is one of those truths, which to a correct and unprejudiced mind, carries its own evidence along with it; and may be obscured, but cannot be made plainer by argument or reasoning. It rests upon axioms as simple as they are universal. The *means* ought to be proportioned to the *end*; the persons, from whose agency the attainment of any *end* is expected, ought to possess the *means* by which it is to be attained.

Whether there ought to be a Fœderal Government intrusted with the care of the common defence, is a question in the first instance open to discussion; but the moment it is decided in the affirmative, it will follow, that that government ought to be cloathed with all the powers requisite to the complete execution of its trust. And unless it can be shewn, that the circumstances which may affect the public safety are reducible within certain determinate limits; unless the contrary of this position can be fairly and rationally disputed, it must be admitted, as a necessary consequence, that there can be no limitation of that authority, which is to provide for the defence and protection of the community, in any matter essential to its efficacy; that is, in any matter essential to the *formation, direction* or *support* of the NATIONAL FORCES.

Defective as the present Confederation has been proved to be, this principle appears to have been fully recognized by the framers of it; though they have not made proper or adequate provision for its exercise. Congress have an unlimited discretion to make requisitions of men and money—to govern the army and navy—to direct their operations. As their requisitions were made constitutionally binding upon the States, who are in fact under the most solemn obligations to furnish the supplies required of them, the intention evidently was, that the United States should command whatever resources were by them judged requisite to "the common defence and general welfare." It was presumed that a sense of their true interests, and a regard to the dictates of good faith, would be found sufficient pledges for the punctual performance of the duty of the members to the Fœderal Head.

The experiment has, however demonstrated, that this expectation was ill founded and illusory; and the observations made under the last head, will, I imagine, have sufficed to convince the impartial and discerning, that there is an absolute necessity for an entire change in the first principles of the system: That if we are in earnest about giving the Union energy and duration, we must abandon the vain project of legislating upon the States in their collective capacities: We must extend the laws of the Fœderal Government to the individual citizens of America: We must discard the fallacious scheme of quotas and requisitions, as equally impracticable and unjust. The result from all this is, that the Union ought to be invested with full power to levy troops; to build and equip fleets, and to raise the revenues, which will be required for the formation and support of an army and navy, in the customary and ordinary modes practiced in other governments.

If the circumstances of our country are such, as to demand a compound instead of a simple, a confederate instead of a sole government, the essential point which will remain to be adjusted, will be to discriminate the OBJECTS, as far as it can be done, which shall appertain to the different provinces or departments of power; allowing to each the most ample authority for fulfilling the objects committed to its charge. Shall the Union be constituted the guardian of the common safety? Are fleets and armies and revenues necessary to this pur-

pose? The government of the Union must be empow-
ered to pass all laws, and to make all regulations which
have relation to them. The same must be the case, in
respect to commerce, and to every other matter to
which its jurisdiction is permitted to extend. Is the
administration of justice between the citizens of the
same State, the proper department of the local governments? These must possess all the authorities which
are connected with this object, and with every other
that may be allotted to their particular cognizance and
direction. Not to confer in each case a degree of power,
commensurate to the end, would be to violate the most
obvious rules of prudence and propriety, and improvi-
dently to trust the great interests of the nation to
hands, which are disabled from managing them with
vigour and success.

Who so likely to make suitable provisions for the
public defence, as that body to which the guardianship
of the public safety is confided—which, as the center
of information, will best understand the extent and
urgency of the dangers that threaten—as the representative of the WHOLE will feel itself most deeply interested in the preservation of every part—which, from
the responsibility implied in the duty assigned to it,
will be most sensibly impressed with the necessity of
proper exertions—and which, by the extension of its
authority throughout the States, can alone establish
uniformity and concert in the plans and measures, by
which the common safety is to be secured? Is there
not a manifest inconsistency in devolving upon the
Fœderal Government the care of the general defence,
and leaving in the State governments the *effective* powers, by which it is to be provided for? Is not a want of

co-operation the infallible consequence of such a system? And will not weakness, disorder, an undue distribution of the burthens and calamities of war, an unnecessary and intolerable increase of expence, be its natural and inevitable concomitants? Have we not had unequivocal experience of its effects in the course of the revolution, which we have just accomplished?

Every view we may take of the subject, as candid enquirers after truth, will serve to convince us, that it is both unwise and dangerous to deny the Fœderal Government an unconfined authority, as to all those objects which are intrusted to its management. It will indeed deserve the most vigilant and careful attention of the people, to see that it be modelled in such a manner, as to admit of its being safely vested with the requisite powers. If any plan which has been, or may be offered to our consideration, should not, upon a dispassionate inspection, be found to answer this description, it ought to be rejected. A government, the Constitution of which renders it unfit to be trusted with all the powers, which a free people *ought to delegate to any government*, would be an unsafe and improper depository of the NATIONAL INTERESTS, wherever THESE can with propriety be confided, the co-incident powers may safely accompany them. This is the true result of all just reasoning upon the subject. And the adversaries of the plan, promulgated by the Convention, ought to have confined themselves to showing that the internal structure of the proposed government, was such as to render it unworthy of the confidence of the people. They ought not to have wandered into inflammatory declamations, and unmeaning cavils about the extent of the powers. The POWERS are not too extensive for the OBJECTS of Fœderal administration, or in other words, for the management of our NATIONAL INTERESTS; nor can any satisfactory argument be framed to shew that they are chargeable with such an excess. If it be true, as has been insinuated by some of the writers on the other side, that the difficulty arises from the nature of the thing, and that the extent of the country will not permit us to form a government, in which such ample powers can safely be reposed, it would prove that we ought to contract our views, and resort to the expedient of separate Confederacies, which will move within more practicable spheres. For the absurdity must continually stare us in the face of confiding to a government, the direction of the most essential national interests, without daring to trust it with the authorities which are indispensable to their proper and efficient management. Let us not attempt to reconcile contradictions, but firmly embrace a rational alternative.

I trust, however, that the impracticability of one general system cannot be shewn. I am greatly mistaken, if any thing of weight, has yet been advanced of this tendency; and I flatter myself, that the observations which have been made in the course of these papers, have sufficed to place the reverse of that position in as clear a light as any matter still in the womb of time and experience can be susceptible of. This at all events must be evident, that the very difficulty itself drawn from the extent of the country, is the strongest argument in favor of an energetic government; for any other can certainly never preserve the Union of so large an empire. If we embrace the tenets of those, who oppose the adoption of the proposed Constitution, as the standard of our political creed, we cannot fail to verify

the gloomy doctrines, which predict the impracticability of a national system, pervading the entire limits of
the present Confederacy.

PUBLIUS.

THE FEDERALIST NO. 39

JAMES MADISON

JANUARY 16, 1788

To the People of the State of New York.

The last paper having concluded the observations
which were meant to introduce a candid survey of the
plan of government reported by the Convention, we
now proceed to the execution of that part of our undertaking. The first question that offers itself is, whether
the general form and aspect of the government be
strictly republican? It is evident that no other form
would be reconcileable with the genius of the people of
America; with the fundamental principles of the revolution; or with that honorable determination, which
animates every votary of freedom, to rest all our political experiments on the capacity of mankind for self-
government. If the plan of the Convention therefore be
found to depart from the republican character, its advocates must abandon it as no longer defensible.

What then are the distinctive characters of the republican form? Were an answer to this question to be
sought, not by recurring to principles, but in the application of the term by political writers, to the consti-

tutions of different States, no satisfactory one would ever be found. Holland, in which no particle of the supreme authority is derived from the people, has passed almost universally under the denomination of a republic. The same title has been bestowed on Venice, where absolute power over the great body of the people, is exercised in the most absolute manner, by a small body of hereditary nobles. Poland, which is a mixture of aristocracy and of monarchy in their worst forms, has been dignified with the same appellation. The government of England, which has one republican branch only, combined with a hereditery aristocracy and monarchy, has with equal impropriety been frequently placed on the list of republics. These examples, which are nearly as dissimilar to each other as to a genuine republic, shew the extreme inaccuracy with which the term has been used in political disquisitions.

If we resort for a criterion, to the different principles on which different forms of government are established, we may define a republic to be, or at least may bestow that name on, a government which derives all its powers directly or indirectly from the great body of the people; and is administered by persons holding their offices during pleasure, for a limited period, or during good behaviour. It is *essential* to such a government, that it be derived from the great body of the society, not from an inconsiderable proportion, or a favored class of it; otherwise a handful of tyrannical nobles, exercising their oppressions by a delegation of their powers, might aspire to the rank of republicans, and claim for their government the honorable title of republic. It is *sufficient* for such a government, that the persons administering it be appointed, either directly or indirectly, by the people; and that they hold their appointments by either of the tenures just specified; otherwise every government in the United States, as well as every other popular government that has been or can be well organized or well executed, would be degraded from the republican character. According to the Constitution of every State in the Union, some or other of the officers of government are appointed indirectly only by the people. According to most of them the chief magistrate himself is so appointed. And according to one, this mode of appointment is extended to one of the coordinate branches of the legislature. According to all the Constitutions also, the tenure of the highest offices is extended to a definite period, and in many instances, both within the legislative and executive departments, to a period of years. According to the provisions of most of the constitutions, again, as well as according to the most respectable and received opinions on the subject, the members of the judiciary department are to retain their offices by the firm tenure of good behaviour.

On comparing the Constitution planned by the Convention, with the standard here fixed, we perceive at once that it is in the most rigid sense conformable to it. The House of Representatives, like that of one branch at least of all the State Legislatures, is elected immediately by the great body of the people. The Senate, like the present Congress, and the Senate of Maryland, derives its appointment indirectly from the people. The President is indirectly derived from the choice of the people, according to the example in most of the States. Even the judges, with all other officers of the Union, will, as in the several States, be the choice, though a remote choice, of the people themselves. The duration of the appointments is equally conformable to the republican standard, and to the model of the State Constitutions. The House of Representatives is periodically elective as in all the States: and for the period of two years as in the State of South-Carolina. The Senate is elective for the period of six years; which is but one year more than the period of the Senate of Maryland; and but two more than that of the Senates of New York and Virginia. The President is to continue in office for the period of four years; as in New-York and Delaware, the chief magistrate is elected for three years, and in South-Carolina for two years. In the other States the election is annual. In several of the States however, no constitutional provision is made for the impeachment of the Chief Magistrate. And in Delaware and Virginia, he is not impeachable till out of office. The President of the United States is impeachable at any time during his continuance in office. The tenure by which the Judges are to hold their places, is, as it unquestionably ought to be, that of good behaviour. The tenure of the ministerial offices generally will be a subject of legal regulation, conformably to the reason of the case, and the example of the State Constitutions.

Could any further proof be required of the republican complextion of this system, the most decisive one might be found in its absolute prohibition of titles of nobility, both under the Federal and the State Governments; and in its express guarantee of the republican form to each of the latter.

But it was not sufficient, say the adversaries of the proposed Constitution, for the Convention to adhere to the republican form. They ought, with equal care, to have preserved the *federal* form, which regards the union as a *confederacy* of sovereign States; instead of which, they have framed a *national* government, which regards the union as a *consolidation* of the States. And it is asked by what authority this bold and radical innovation was undertaken. The handle which has been made of this objection requires, that it should be examined with some precision.

Without enquiring into the accuracy of the distinction on which the objection is founded, it will be necessary to a just estimate of its force, first to ascertain the real character of the government in question; secondly, to enquire how far the Convention were authorised to propose such a government; and thirdly, how far the duty they owed to their country, could supply any defect of regular authority.

First. In order to ascertain the real character of the government it may be considered in relation to the foundation on which it is to be established; to the sources from which its ordinary powers are to be drawn; to the operation of those powers; to the extent of them; and to the authority by which future changes in the government are to be introduced.

On examining the first relation, it appears on one hand that the Constitution is to be founded on the assent and ratification of the people of America, given by deputies elected for the special purpose; but on the other, that this assent and ratification is to be given by the people, not as individuals composing one entire nation; but as composing the distinct and independent States to which they respectively belong. It is to be the assent and ratification of the several States, derived,

from the supreme authority in each State, the authority of the people themselves. The act therefore establishing the Constitution, will not be a *national* but a
federal act.

That it will be a federal and not a national act, as
these terms are understood by the objectors, the act of
the people as forming so many independent States, not
as forming one aggregate nation, is obvious from this
single consideration that it is to result neither from the
decision of a *majority* of the people of the Union, nor
from that of a *majority* of the States. It must result from
the *unanimous* assent of the several States that are parties to it, differing no other wise from their ordinary
assent than in its being expressed, not by the legislative authority, but by that of the people themselves.
Were the people regarded in this transaction as forming one nation, the will of the majority of the whole
people of the United States, would bind the minority;
in the same manner as the majority in each State must
bind the minority; and the will of the majority must
be determined either by a comparison of the individual
votes; or by considering the will of a majority of the
States, as evidence of the will of a majority of the people of the United States. Neither of these rules has been
adopted. Each State in ratifying the Constitution, is
considered as a sovereign body independent of all others, and only to be bound by its own voluntary act. In
this relation then the new Constitution will, if established, be a *federal* and not a *national* Constitution.

The next relation is to the sources from which the
ordinary powers of government are to be derived. The
house of representatives will derive its powers from
the people of America, and the people will be repre-

sented in the same proportion, and on the same principle, as they are in the Legislature of a particular State.
So far the Government is *national* not *federal*. The
Senate on the other hand will derive its powers from
the States, as political and co-equal societies; and
these will be represented on the principle of equality
in the Senate, as they now are in the existing Congress. So far the government is *federal*, not *national*.
The executive power will be derived from a very compound source. The immediate election of the President
is to be made by the States in their political characters.
The votes allotted to them, are in a compound ratio,
which considers them partly as distinct and co-equal
societies; partly as unequal members of the same society. The eventual election, again is to be made by that
branch of the Legislature which consists of the
national representatives; but in this particular act, they
are to be thrown into the form of individual delega-
tions from so many distinct and co-equal bodies politic. From this aspect of the Government, it appears to
be of a mixed character presenting at least as many
federal as *national* features.

The difference between a federal and national Government as it relates to the *operation of the Government*
is supposed to consist in this, that in the former, the
powers operate on the political bodies composing the
confederacy, in their political capacities: In the latter,
on the individual citizens, composing the nation, in
their individual capacities. On trying the Constitution
by this criterion, it falls under the *national*, not the
federal character; though perhaps not so compleatly, as
has been understood. In several cases and particularly
in the trial of controversies to which States may be par-

ties, they must be viewed and proceeded against in their collective and political capacities only. So far the national countenance of the Government on this side seems to be disfigured by a few federal features. But this blemish is perhaps unavoidable in any plan; and the operation of the Government on the people in their individual capacities, in its ordinary and most essential proceedings, may on the whole designate it in this relation a *national* Government.

But if the Government be national with regard to the *operation* of its powers, it changes its aspect again when we contemplate it in relation to the *extent* of its powers. The idea of a national Government involves in it, not only an authority over the individual citizens; but an indefinite supremacy over all persons and things, so far as they are objects of lawful Government. Among a people consolidated into one nation, this supremacy is compleatly vested in the national Legislature. Among communities united for particular purposes, it is vested partly in the general, and partly in the municipal Legislatures. In the former case, all local authorities are subordinate to the supreme; and may be controuled, directed or abolished by it at pleasure. In the latter the local or municipal authorities form distinct and independent portions of the supremacy, no more subject within their respective spheres to the general authority, than the general authority is subject to them, within its own sphere. In this relation then the proposed Government cannot be deemed a *national* one; since its jurisdiction extends to certain enumerated objects only, and leaves to the several States a residuary and inviolable sovereignty over all other objects. It is true that in controversies relating to the boundary between the two jurisdictions, the tribunal which is ultimately to decide, is to be established under the general Government. But this does not change the principle of the case. The decision is to be impartially made, according to the rules of the Constitution; and all the usual and most effectual precautions are taken to secure this impartiality. Some such tribunal is clearly essential to prevent an appeal to the sword, and a dissolution of the compact; and that it ought to be established under the general, rather than under the local Governments; or to speak more properly, that it could be safely established under the first alone, is a position not likely to be combated.

If we try the Constitution by its last relation, to the authority by which amendments are to be made, we find it neither wholly *national*, nor wholly *federal*. Were it wholly national, the supreme and ultimate authority would reside in the *majority* of the people of the Union; and this authority would be competent at all times, like that of a majority of every national society, to alter or abolish its established Government. Were it wholly federal on the other hand, the concurrence of each State in the Union would be essential to every alteration that would be binding on all. The mode provided by the plan of the Convention is not founded on either of these principles. In requiring more than a majority, and particularly, in computing the proportion by *States*, not by *citizens*, it departs from the *national*, and advances towards the *federal* character: In rendering the concurrence of less than the whole number of States sufficient, it loses again the *federal*, and partakes of the *national* character.

The proposed Constitution therefore is in strictness

neither a national nor a federal constitution; but a composition of both. In its foundation, it is federal, not national; in the sources from which the ordinary powers of the Government are drawn, it is partly federal, and partly national: in the operation of these powers, it is national, not federal: In the extent of them again, it is federal, not national: And finally, in the authoritative mode of introducing amendments, it is neither wholly federal, nor wholly national.

PUBLIUS.

THE FEDERALIST NO. 45

JAMES MADISON

JANUARY 26, 1788

To the People of the State of New York.

Having shewn that no one of the powers transferred to the federal Government is unnecessary or improper, the next question to be considered is whether the whole mass of them will be dangerous to the portion of authority left in the several States.

The adversaries to the plan of the Convention instead of considering in the first place what degree of power was absolutely necessary for the purposes of the federal Government, have exhausted themselves in a secondary enquiry into the possible consequences of the proposed degree of power, to the Governments of the particular States. But if the Union, as has been shewn, be essential, to the security of the people of

America against foreign danger; if it be essential to their security against contentions and wars among the different States; if it be essential to guard them against those violent and oppressive factions which embitter the blessings of liberty, and against those military establishments which must gradually poison its very fountain; if, in a word the Union be essential to the happiness of the people of America, is it not preposterous, to urge as an objection to a government without which the objects of the Union cannot be attained, that such a Government may derogate from the importance of the Governments of the individual States? Was then the American revolution effected, was the American confederacy formed, was the precious blood of thousands spilt, and the hard earned substance of millions lavished, not that the people of America should enjoy peace, liberty and safety; but that the Governments of the individual States, that particular municipal establishments, might enjoy a certain extent of power, and be arrayed with certain dignities and attributes of sovereignty? We have heard of the impious doctrine in the old world that the people were made for kings, not kings for the people. Is the same doctrine to be revived in the new, in another shape, that the solid happiness of the people is to be sacrificed to the views of political institutions of a different form? It is too early for politicians to presume on our forgetting that the public good, the real welfare of the great body of the people is the supreme object to be pursued; and that no form of Government whatever, has any other value, than as it may be fitted for the attainment of this object. Were the plan of the Convention adverse to the public happiness, my voice would be, reject the plan. Were the

Union itself inconsistent with the public happiness, it would be, abolish the Union. In like manner as far as the sovereignty of the States cannot be reconciled to the happiness of the people, the voice of every good citizen must be, let the former be sacrificed to the latter. How far the sacrifice is necessary, has been shewn. How far the unsacrificed residue will be endangered, is the question before us.

Several important considerations have been touched in the course of these papers, which discountenance the supposition that the operation of the federal Government will by degrees prove fatal to the State Governments. The more I revolve the subject the more fully I am persuaded that the balance is much more likely to be disturbed by the preponderancy of the last than of the first scale.

We have seen in all the examples of antient and modern confederacies, the strongest tendency continually betraying itself in the members to despoil the general Government of its authorities, with a very ineffectual capacity in the latter to defend itself against the encroachments. Although in most of these examples, the system has been so dissimilar from that under consideration, as greatly to weaken any inference concerning the latter from the fate of the former; yet as the States will retain under the proposed Constitution a very extensive portion of active sovereignty, the inference ought not to be wholly disregarded. In the Achaean league, it is probable that the federal head had a degree and species of power, which gave it a considerable likeness to the government framed by the Convention. The Lycian confederacy, as far as its principles and form are transmitted, must have borne a still greater analogy to it. Yet history does not inform us that either of them ever degenerated or tended to degenerate into one consolidated government. On the contrary, we know that the ruin of one of them proceeded from the incapacity of the federal authority to prevent the dissentions, and finally the disunion of the subordinate authorities. These cases are the more worthy of our attention, as the external causes by which the component parts were pressed together, were much more numerous and powerful than in our case; and consequently, less powerful ligaments within, would be sufficient to bind the members to the head, and to each other.

In the feudal system we have seen a similar propensity exemplified. Notwithstanding the want of proper sympathy in every instance between the local sovereigns and the people, and the sympathy in some instances between the general sovereign and the latter; it usually happened that the local sovereigns prevailed in the rivalship for encroachments. Had no external dangers, enforced internal harmony and subordination; and particularly had the local sovereigns possessed the affections of the people, the great kingdoms in Europe, would at this time consist of as many independent princes as there were formerly feudatory barons.

The State Governments will have the advantage of the federal Government, whether we compare them in respect to the immediate dependence of the one or the other; to the weight of personal influence which each side will possess; to the powers respectively vested in them; to the predilection and probable support of the people; to the disposition and faculty of resisting and frustrating the measures of each other.

The State Governments may be regarded as constituent and essential parts of the federal Government; whilst the latter is nowise essential to the operation or organisation of the former. Without the intervention of the State Legislatures, the President of the United States cannot be elected at all. They must in all cases have a great share in his appointment, and will perhaps in most cases of themselves determine it. The Senate will be elected absolutely and exclusively by the State Legislatures. Even the House of Representatives, though drawn immediately from the people, will be chosen very much under the influence of that class of men, whose influence over the people obtains for themselves an election into the State Legislatures. Thus each of the principal branches of the federal Government will owe its existence more or less to the favor of the State Governments, and must consequently feel a dependence, which is much more likely to beget a disposition too obsequious, than too overbearing towards them. On the other side, the component parts of the State Governments will in no instance be indebted for their appointment to the direct agency of the federal government, and very little if at all, to the local influence of its members.

The number of individuals employed under the Constitution of the United States, will be much smaller, than the number employed under the particular States. There will consequently be less of personal influence on the side of the former, than of the latter. The members of the legislative, executive and judiciary departments of thirteen and more States; the justices of peace, officers of militia, ministerial officers of justice, with all the county corporation and town-officers, for three millions and more of people, intermixed and having particular acquaintance with every class and circle of people, must exceed beyond all proportion, both in number and influence, those of every description who will be employed in the administration of the federal system. Compare the members of the three great departments, of the thirteen States, excluding from the judiciary department the justices of peace, with the members of the corresponding departments of the single Government of the Union; compare the militia officers of three millions of people, with the military and marine officers of any establishment which is within the compass of probability, or I may add, of possibility, and in this view alone, we may pronounce the advantage of the States to be decisive. If the federal Government is to have collectors of revenue, the State Governments will have theirs also. And as those of the former will be principally on the sea-coast, and not very numerous; whilst those of the latter will be spread over the face of the country, and will be very numerous, the advantage in this view also lies on the same side. It is true that the confederacy is to possess, and may exercise, the power of collecting internal as well as external taxes throughout the States: But it is probable that this power will not be resorted to, except for supplemental purposes of revenue; that an option will then be given to the States to supply their quotas by previous collections of their own; and that the eventual collection under the immediate authority of the Union, will generally be made by the officers, and according to the rules, appointed by the several States. Indeed it is extremely probable that in other instances, particularly in the organisation of the judicial power, the officers of the States will be cloathed with the correspondent authority of the Union. Should it happen however that separate collectors of internal revenue should be appointed under the federal Government, the influence of the whole number would not be a comparison with that of the multitude of State officers in the opposite scale. Within every district, to which a federal collector would be allotted, there would not be less than thirty or forty or even more officers of different descriptions and many of them persons of character and weight, whose influence would lie on the side of the State.

The powers delegated by the proposed Constitution to the Federal Government, are few and defined. Those which are to remain in the State Governments are numerous and indefinite. The former will be exercised principally on external objects, as war, peace, negociation, and foreign commerce; with which last the power of taxation will for the most part be connected. The powers reserved to the several States will extend to all the objects, which, in the ordinary course of affairs, concern the lives, liberties and properties of the people; and the internal order, improvement, and prosperity of the State.

The operations of the Federal Government will be most extensive and important in times of war and danger; those of the State Governments, in times of peace and security. As the former periods will probably bear a small proportion to the latter, the State Governments will here enjoy another advantage over the Federal Government. The more adequate indeed the federal powers may be rendered to the national defence, the less frequent will be those scenes of danger which might favour their ascendency over the governments of the particular States.

If the new Constitution be examined with accuracy and candour, it will be found that the change which it proposes, consists much less in the addition of NEW POWERS to the Union, than in the invigoration of its ORIGINAL POWERS. The regulation of commerce, it is true, is a new power; but that seems to be an addition which few oppose, and from which no apprehensions are entertained. The powers relating to war and peace, armies and fleets, treaties and finance, with the other more considerable powers, are all vested in the existing Congress by the articles of Confederation. The proposed change does not enlarge these powers; it only substitutes a more effectual mode of administering them. The change relating to taxation, may be regarded as the most important: And yet the present Congress have as compleat authority to REQUIRE of the States indefinite supplies of money for the common defence and general welfare, as the future Congress will have to require them of individual citizens; and the latter will be no more bound than the States themselves have been, to pay the quotas respectively taxed on them. Had the States complied punctually with the articles of confederation, or could their compliance have been enforced by as peaceable means as may be used with success towards single persons, our past experience is very far from countenancing an opinion that the State Governments would have lost their constitutional powers, and have gradually undergone an entire consolidation. To maintain that such an event would have ensued, would be to say at once, that the existence of the State Governments is incompatible with any system whatever that accomplishes the essential purposes of the Union.

PUBLIUS.

THE FEDERALIST NO. 46

JAMES MADISON

JANUARY 29, 1788

To the People of the State of New York.

Resuming the subject of the last paper, I proceed to enquire whether the Fœderal Government or the State Governments will have the advantage with regard to the predilection and support of the people. Notwithstanding the different modes in which they are appointed, we must consider both of them, as substantially dependent on the great body of the citizens of the United States. I assume this position here as it respects the first, reserving the proofs for another place. The Fœderal and State Governments are in fact but different agents and trustees of the people, instituted with different powers, and designated for different purposes. The adversaries of the Constitution seem to have lost sight of the people altogether in their reasonings on this subject; and to have viewed these different establishments, not only as mutual rivals and enemies, but as uncontrouled by any common superior in their efforts to usurp the authorities of each other. These gentlemen must here be reminded of their error. They must be told that the ultimate authority, wherever the derivative may be found, resides in the people alone; and that it will not depend merely on the comparative ambition or address of the different governments, whether either, or which of them, will be able to enlarge its sphere of jurisdiction at the expence of the other. Truth no less than decency requires, that the event in every case, should be supposed to depend on the sentiments and sanction of their common constituents.

Many considerations, besides those suggested on a former occasion, seem to place it beyond doubt, that the first and most natural attachment of the people will be to the governments of their respective States. Into the administration of these, a greater number of individuals will expect to rise. From the gift of these a greater number of offices and emoluments will flow. By the superintending care of these, all the more domestic, and personal interests of the people will be regulated and provided for. With the affairs of these, the people will be more familiarly and minutely conversant. And with the members of these, will a greater proportion of the people have the ties of personal acquaintance and friendship, and of family and party attachments; on the side of these therefore the popular bias, may well be expected most strongly to incline.

Experience speaks the same language in this case. The fœderal administration, though hitherto very defective, in comparison with what may be hoped under a better system, had during the war, and particularly, whilst the independent fund of paper emissions was in credit, an activity and importance as great as it can well have, in any future circumstances whatever. It was engaged too in a course of measures, which had for their object, the protection of every thing that was dear, and the acquisition of every thing that could be desireable to the people at large. It was nevertheless, invariably found, after the transient enthusiasm for the early Congresses was over, that the attention and attachment of the people were turned anew to their own particular government; that the Fœderal Council, was at no time the idol of popular favor; and that opposition to proposed enlargements of its powers and importance, was the side usually taken by the men who wished to build their political consequence on the prepossessions of their fellow citizens.

If therefore, as has been elsewhere remarked, the people should in future become more partial to the fœderal than to the State governments, the change can only result, from such manifest and irresistible proofs of a better administration, as will overcome all their antecedent propensities. And in that case, the people ought not surely to be precluded from giving most of their confidence where they may discover it to be most due: But even in that case, the State governments could have little to apprehend, because it is only within a certain sphere, that the fœderal power can, in the nature of things, be advantageously administered.

The remaining points on which I proposed to compare the fœderal and State governments, are the disposition, and the faculty they may respectively possess, to resist and frustrate the measures of each other.

It has been already proved, that the members of the fœderal will be more dependent on the members of the State governments, than the latter will be on the former. It has appeared also, that the prepossessions of the people on whom both will depend, will be more on the side of the State governments, than of the Fœderal Government. So far as the disposition of each, towards the other, may be influenced by these causes, the State governments must clearly have the advantage. But in a distinct and very important point of view, the advantage will lie on the same side. The prepossessions which the members themselves will carry into the Fœderal Government, will generally be favorable to the States; whilst it will rarely happen, that the members of the State governments will carry into the public councils, a bias in favor of the general government. A local spirit will infallibly prevail much more in the members of the Congress, than a national spirit will prevail in the Legislatures of the particular States. Every one knows that a great proportion of the errors committed by the State Legislatures proceeds from the disposition of the members to sacrifice the comprehensive and permanent interest of the State, to the particular and separate views of the counties or districts in which they reside. And if they do not sufficiently enlarge their policy to embrace the collective welfare of their particular State, how can it be imagined, that they will make the aggregate prosperity of the Union, and the dignity and respectability of its government, the objects of their affections and consultations? For the same reason, that the members of the State Legislatures, will be unlikely to attach themselves sufficiently to national objects, the members of the Fœderal Legislature will be likely to attach themselves too much to local objects. The States will be to the latter, what counties and towns are to the former. Measures will too often be decided according to their probable effect, not on the national prosperity and happiness, but on the prejudices, interests and pursuits of the governments and people of the individual States. What is the spirit that has in general characterized the proceedings of Congress? A perusal of their journals as well as the candid acknowledgments of such as have had a seat in that assembly, will inform us, that the members have but too frequently displayed the character, rather of partizans of their respective States, than of impartial guardians of a common interest; that whereon one occasion improper sacrifices have been made of local considerations to the aggrandizement of the Fœderal Government; the great interests of the nation have suffered on an hundred, from an undue attention to the local prejudices, interests and views of the particular States. I mean not by these reflections to insinuate, that the new Fœderal Government will not embrace a more enlarged plan of policy than the existing government may have pursued, much less that its views will be as confined as those of the State Legislatures; but only that it will partake sufficiently of the spirit of both, to be disinclined to invade the rights of the individual States, or the prerogatives of their governments. The motives on the part of the State governments, to augment their prerogatives by defalcations from the Fœderal Government, will be overruled by no reciprocal predispositions in the members.

Were it admitted however that the Fœderal Government may feel an equal disposition with the State governments to extend its power beyond the due limits, the latter would still have the advantage in the means of defeating such encroachments. If an act of a particular

State, though unfriendly to the national government, be generally popular in that State, and should not too grossly violate the oaths of the State officers, it is executed immediately and of course, by means on the spot, and depending on the State alone. The opposition of the Fœderal Government, or the interposition of Fœderal officers, would but inflame the zeal of all parties on the side of the State, and the evil could not be prevented or repaired, if at all, without the employment of means which must always be resorted to with reluctance and difficulty. On the other hand, should an unwarrantable measure of the Fœderal Government be unpopular in particular States, which would seldom fail to be the case, or even a warrantable measure be so, which may sometimes be the case, the means of opposition to it are powerful and at hand. The disquietude of the people, their repugnance and perhaps refusal to co-operate with the officers of the Union, the frowns of the executive magistracy of the State, the embarrassments created by legislative devices, which would often be added on such occasions, would oppose in any State difficulties not to be despised; would form in a large State very serious impediments, and where the sentiments of several adjoining States happened to be in unison, would present obstructions which the Fœderal Government would hardly be willing to encounter.

But ambitious encroachments of the Fœderal Government, on the authority of the State governments, would not excite the opposition of a single State or of a few States only. They would be signals of general alarm. Every Government would espouse the common cause. A correspondence would be opened. Plans of resistance would be concerted. One spirit would animate and conduct the whole. The same combination in short would result from an apprehension of the fœderal, as was produced by the dread of a foreign yoke; and unless the projected innovations should be voluntarily renounced, the same appeal to a trial of force would be made in the one case, as was made in the other. But what degree of madness could ever drive the Fœderal Government to such an extremity? In the contest with Great Britain, one part of the empire was employed against the other. The more numerous part invaded the rights of the less numerous part. The attempt was unjust and unwise; but it was not in speculation absolutely chimerical. But what would be the contest in the case we are supposing? Who would be the parties? A few representatives of the people, would be opposed to the people themselves; or rather one set of representatives would be contending against thirteen sets of representatives, with the whole body of their common constituents on the side of the latter.

The only refuge left for those who prophecy the downfall of the State Governments, is the visionary supposition that the Fœderal Government may previously accumulate a military force for the projects of ambition. The reasonings contained in these papers must have been employed to little purpose indeed, if it could be necessary now to disprove the reality of this danger. That the people and the States should for a sufficient period of time elect an uninterrupted succession of men ready to betray both; that the traitors should throughout this period, uniformly and systematically pursue some fixed plan for the extension of the military establishment; that the governments and the people of the States should silently and patiently behold the gathering storm, and continue to supply the materials, until it should be prepared to burst on their own heads, must appear to every one more like the incoherent dreams of a delirious jealousy, or the misjudged exaggerations of a counterfeit zeal, than like the sober apprehensions of genuine patriotism. Extravagant as the supposition is, let it however be made. Let a regular army, fully equal to the resources of the country be formed; and let it be entirely at the devotion of the Fœderal Government; still it would not be going too far to say, that the State Governments with the people on their side would be able to repel the danger. The highest number to which, according to the best computation, a standing army can be carried in any country, does not exceed one hundredth part of the whole number of souls; or one twenty-fifth part of the number able to bear arms. This proportion would not yield in the United States an army of more than twenty-five or thirty thousand men. To these would be opposed a militia amounting to near half a million of citizens with arms in their hands, officered by men chosen from among themselves, fighting for their common liberties, and united and conducted by governments possessing their affections and confidence. It may well be doubted whether a militia thus circumstanced could ever be conquered by such a proportion of regular troops. Those who are best acquainted with the late successful resistance of this country against the British arms will be most inclined to deny the possibility of it. Besides the advantage of being armed, which the Americans possess over the people of almost every other nation, the existence of subordinate governments to which the people are attached, and by which the militia officers are appointed, forms a barrier against the enterprizes of ambition, more insurmountable than any which a simple government of any form can admit of. Notwithstanding the military establishments in the several kingdoms of Europe, which are carried as far as the public resources will bear, the governments are afraid to trust the people with arms. And it is not certain that with this aid alone, they would not be able to shake off their yokes. But were the people to possess the additional advantages of local governments chosen by themselves, who could collect the national will, and direct the national force; and of officers appointed out of the militia, by these governments and attached both to them and to the militia, it may be affirmed with the greatest assurance, that the throne of every tyranny in Europe would be speedily overturned, in spite of the legions which surround it. Let us not insult the free and gallant citizens of America with the suspicion that they would be less able to defend the rights of which they would be in actual possession, than the debased subjects of arbitrary power would be to rescue theirs from the hands of their oppressors. Let us rather no longer insult them with the supposition, that they can ever reduce themselves to the necessity of making the experiment, by a blind and tame submission to the long train of insidious measures, which must precede and produce it.

The argument under the present head may be put into a very concise form, which appears altogether conclusive. Either the mode in which the Fœderal Government is to be constructed will render it sufficiently dependant on the people, or it will not. On the first supposition, it will be restrained by that dependence from forming schemes obnoxious to their constituents. On the other supposition it will not possess the confidence of the people, and its schemes of usurpation will be easily defeated by the State Governments; who will be supported by the people.

On summing up the considerations stated in this and the last paper, they seem to amount to the most convincing evidence, that the powers proposed to be lodged in the Fœderal Government, are as little formidable to those reserved to the individual States, as they are indispensibly necessary to accomplish the purposes of the Union; and that all those alarms which have been sounded, of a meditated or consequential annihilation of the State Governments, must, on the most favorable interpretation, be ascribed to the chimerical fears of the authors of them.

PUBLIUS.

THE FEDERALIST NO. 47

JAMES MADISON

JANUARY 30, 1788

To the People of the State of New York.

Having reviewed the general form of the proposed government, and the general mass of power allotted to it: I proceed to examine the particular structure of this government, and the distribution of this mass of power among its constituent parts.

One of the principal objections inculcated by the more respectable adversaries to the constitution, is its supposed violation of the political maxim, that the legislative, executive and judiciary departments ought to be separate and distinct. In the structure of the federal government, no regard, it is said, seems to have been paid to this essential precaution in favor of liberty. The several departments of power are distributed and blended in such a manner, as at once to destroy all symmetry and beauty of form; and to expose some of the essential parts of the edifice to the danger of being crushed by the disproportionate weight of other parts.

No political truth is certainly of greater intrinsic value or is stamped with the authority of more enlightened patrons of liberty than that on which the objection is founded. The accumulation of all powers legislative, executive and judiciary in the same hands, whether of one, a few or many, and whether hereditary, self appointed, or elective, may justly be pronounced the very definition of tyranny. Were the federal constitution therefore really chargeable with this accumulation of power or with a mixture of powers having a dangerous tendency to such an accumulation, no further arguments would be necessary to inspire a universal reprobation of the system. I persuade myself however, that it will be made apparent to every one, that the charge cannot be supported, and that the maxim on which it relies, has been totally misconceived and misapplied. In order to form correct ideas on this important subject, it will be proper to investigate the sense, in which the preservation of liberty requires, that the three great departments of power should be separate and distinct.

The oracle who is always consulted and cited on this subject, is the celebrated Montesquieu. If he be not the author of this invaluable precept in the science of politics, he has the merit at least of displaying, and recommending it most effectually to the attention of mankind. Let us endeavour in the first place to ascertain his meaning on this point.

The British constitution was to Montesquieu, what Homer has been to the didactic writers on epic poetry. As the latter have considered the work of the immortal Bard, as the perfect model from which the principles and rules of the epic art were to be drawn, and by which all similar works were to be judged; so this great political critic appears to have viewed the constitution of England, as the standard, or to use his own expression, as the mirrour of political liberty; and to have delivered in the form of elementary truths, the several characteristic principles of that particular system. That we may be sure then not to mistake his meaning in this case, let us recur to the source from which the maxim was drawn.

On the slightest view of the British constitution we must perceive, that the legislative, executive and judiciary departments are by no means totally separate and distinct from each other. The executive magistrate forms an integral part of the legislative authority. He alone has the prerogative of making treaties with foreign sovereigns, which when made have, under certain limitations, the force of legislative acts. All the members of the judiciary department are appointed by him; can be removed by him on the address of the two Houses of Parliament, and form, when he pleases to consult them, one of his constitutional councils. One branch of the legislative department forms also, a great constitutional council to the executive chief; as on another hand, it is the sole depositary of judicial power in cases of impeachment, and is invested with the supreme appellate jurisdiction, in all other cases. The judges again are so far connected with the legislative department, as often to attend and participate in its deliberations, though not admitted to a legislative vote.

From these facts by which Montesquieu was guided it may clearly be inferred, that in saying "there can be no liberty where the legislative and executive powers are united in the same person, or body of magistrates," or "if the power of judging be not separated from the legislative and executive powers," he did not mean that these departments ought to have no *partial agency* in, or no *controul* over the acts of each other. His meaning, as his own words import, and still more conclusively as illustrated by the example in his eye, can amount to no more than this, that where the *whole* power of one department is exercised by the same hands which possess the *whole* power of another department, the fundamental principles of a free constitution, are subverted. This would have been the case in the constitution examined by him, if the King who is the sole executive magistrate, had possessed also the compleat legislative power, or the supreme administration of justice; or if the entire legislative body, had possessed the supreme judiciary, or the supreme executive authority. This however is not among the vices of that constitution. The magistrate in whom the whole executive power resides cannot of himself make a law, though he can put a negative on every law, nor administer justice in person, though he has the appointment of those who do administer it. The judges can exercise no executive prerogative, though they are shoots from the executive stock, nor any legislative function, though they may be advised with by the legislative councils. The entire legislature, can perform no judiciary act, though by the joint act of two of its branches, the judges may be removed from their offices; and though one of its branches is possessed of the judicial power in the last resort. The entire legislature again can exercise no executive prerogative, though one of its branches constitutes the supreme executive magistracy; and another, on the empeachment of a third, can try and condemn all the subordinate officers in the executive department.

The reasons on which Montesquieu grounds his maxim are a further demonstration of his meaning. "When the legislative and executive powers are united in the same person or body" says he, "there can be no liberty, because apprehensions may arise lest *the same* monarch or senate should *enact* tyrannical laws, to *execute* them in a tyrannical manner." Again "Were the power of judging joined with the legislative, the life and liberty of the subject would be exposed to arbitrary controul, for *the judge* would then be *the legislator.* Were it joined to the executive power, *the judge* might behave with all the violence of *an oppressor.*" Some of these reasons are more fully explained in other passages; but briefly stated as they are here, they sufficiently establish the meaning which we have put on this celebrated maxim of this celebrated author.

If we look into the constitutions of the several states

we find that notwithstanding the emphatical, and in some instances, the unqualified terms in which this axiom has been laid down, there is not a single instance in which the several departments of power have been kept absolutely separate and distinct. New Hampshire, whose constitution was the last formed, seems to have been fully aware of the impossibility and inexpediency of avoiding any mixture whatever of these departments; and has qualified the doctrine by declaring "that the legislative, executive and judiciary powers ought to be kept as separate from, and independent of each other *as the nature of a free government will admit; or as is consistent with that chain of connection, that binds the whole fabric of the constitution in one indissoluble bond of unity and amity.*" Her constitution accordingly mixes these departments in several respects. The senate which is a branch of the legislative department is also a judicial tribunal for the trial of empeachments. The president who is the head of the executive department, is the presiding member also of the senate; and besides an equal vote in all cases, has a casting vote in case of a tie. The executive head is himself eventually elective every year by the legislative department; and his council is every year chosen by and from the members of the same department. Several of the officers of state are also appointed by the legislature. And the members of the judiciary department are appointed by the executive department.

The constitution of Massachusetts has observed a sufficient though less pointed caution in expressing this fundamental article of liberty. It declares "that the legislative department shall never exercise the execu-

tive and judicial powers, or either of them: The executive shall never exercise the legislative and judicial
powers, or either of them: The judicial shall never exercise the legislative and executive powers, or either of
them." This declaration corresponds precisely with the
doctrine of Montesquieu as it has been explained, and
is not in a single point violated by the plan of the Convention. It goes no farther than to prohibit any one of
the entire departments from exercising the powers of
another department. In the very constitution to which
it is prefixed, a partial mixture of powers has been admitted. The Executive Magistrate has a qualified negative on the Legislative body; and the Senate, which is
a part of the Legislature, is a court of impeachment
for members both of the executive and judiciary departments. The members of the judiciary department
again are appointable by the executive department,
and removeable by the same authority, on the address
of the two legislative branches. Lastly, a number of the
officers of government are annually appointed by the
legislative department. As the appointment to offices,
particularly executive offices, is in its nature an executive function, the compilers of the Constitution have
in this last point at least, violated the rule established
by themselves.

I pass over the constitutions of Rhode-Island and
Connecticut, because they were formed prior to the
revolution; and even before the principle under examination had become an object of political attention.

The constitution of New-York contains no declaration on this subject; but appears very clearly to have
been framed with an eye to the danger of improperly
blending the different departments. It gives neverthe-

less to the executive magistrate a partial controul over the legislative department; and what is more, gives a like controul to the judiciary department, and even blends the executive and judiciary departments in the exercise of this controul. In its council of appointment, members of the legislative are associated with the executive authority in the appointment of officers both executive and judiciary. And its court for the trial of impeachments and correction of errors, is to consist of one branch of the legislature and the principal members of the judiciary department.

The constitution of New-Jersey has blended the different powers of government more than any of the preceding. The governor, who is the executive magistrate, is appointed by the legislature; is chancellor and ordinary or surrogate of the state; is a member of the supreme court of appeals, and president with a casting vote, of one of the legislative branches. The same legislative branch acts again as executive council to the governor, and with him constitutes the court of appeals. The members of the judiciary department are appointed by the legislative department, and removeable by one branch of it, on the impeachment of the other.

According to the constitution of Pennsylvania, the president, who is head of the executive department, is annually elected by a vote in which the legislative department predominates. In conjunction with an executive council, he appoints the members of the judiciary department, and forms a court of impeachments for trial of all officers, judiciary as well as executive. The judges of the supreme court, and justices of the peace, seem also to be removeable by the legislature; and the executive power of pardoning in certain cases to be referred to the same department. The members of the executive council are made EX OFFICIO justices of peace throughout the state.

In Delaware, the chief executive magistrate is annually elected by the legislative department. The speakers of the two legislative branches are vice-presidents in the executive department. The executive chief, with six others, appointed three by each of the legislative branches, constitute the supreme court of appeals: He is joined with the legislative department in the appointment of the other judges. Throughout the states it appears that the members of the legislature may at the same time be justices of the peace. In this state, the members of one branch of it are EX OFFICIO justices of peace; as are also the members of the executive council. The principal officers of the executive department are appointed by the legislative; and one branch of the latter forms a court of impeachments. All officers may be removed on address of the legislature.

Maryland has adopted the maxim in the most unqualified terms; declaring that the legislative, executive and judicial powers of government, ought to be forever separate and distinct from each other. Her constitution, notwithstanding makes the executive magistrate appointable by the legislative department; and the members of the judiciary, by the executive department.

The language of Virginia is still more pointed on this subject. Her constitution declares, "that the legislative, executive and judiciary departments, shall be separate and distinct; so that neither exercise the powers properly belonging to the other; nor shall any person exercise the powers of more than one of them at the same time; except that the justices of the county courts shall be eligible to either house of assembly." Yet we find not only this express exception, with respect to the members of the inferior courts; but that the chief magistrate with his executive council are appointable by the legislature; that two members of the latter are triennially displaced at the pleasure of the legislature; and that all the principal offices, both executive and judiciary, are filled by the same department. The executive prerogative of pardon, also is in one case vested in the legislative department.

The constitution of North-Carolina, which declares, "that the legislative, executive and supreme judicial powers of government, ought to be forever separate and distinct from each other," refers at the same time to the legislative department, the appointment not only of the executive chief, but all the principal officers within both that and the judiciary department.

In South-Carolina, the constitution makes the executive magistracy eligible by the legislative department. It gives to the latter also the appointment of the members of the judiciary department, including even justices of the peace and sheriffs; and the appointment of officers in the executive department, down to captains in the army and navy of the state.

In the constitution of Georgia, where it is declared, "that the legislative, executive and judiciary departments shall be separate and distinct, so that neither exercise the powers properly belonging to the other." We find that the executive department is to be filled by appointments of the legislature; and the executive prerogative of pardon, to be finally exercised by the same authority. Even justices of the peace are to be appointed by the legislature.

In citing these cases in which the legislative, executive and judiciary departments, have not been kept totally separate and distinct, I wish not to be regarded as an advocate for the particular organizations of the several state governments. I am fully aware that among the many excellent principles which they exemplify, they carry strong marks of the haste, and still stronger of the inexperience, under which they were framed. It is but too obvious that in some instances, the fundamental principle under consideration has been violated by too great a mixture, and even an actual consolidation of the different powers; and that in no instance has a competent provision been made for maintaining in practice the separation delineated on paper. What I have wished to evince is, that the charge brought against the proposed constitution, of violating a sacred maxim of free government, is warranted neither by the real meaning annexed to that maxim by its author; nor by the sense in which it has hitherto been understood in America. This interesting subject will be resumed in the ensuing paper.

PUBLIUS.

THE FEDERALIST NO. 48

JAMES MADISON

FEBRUARY 1, 1788

To the People of the State of New York.

It was shewn in the last paper, that the political apothegm there examined, does not require that the legislative, executive and judiciary departments should be wholly unconnected with each other. I shall undertake in the next place, to shew that unless these departments be so far connected and blended, as to give to each a constitutional controul over the others, the degree of separation which the maxim requires as essential to a free government, can never in practice, be duly maintained.

It is agreed on all sides, that the powers properly belonging to one of the departments, ought not to be directly and compleatly administered by either of the other departments. It is equally evident, that neither of them ought to possess directly or indirectly, an overruling influence over the others in the administration of their respective powers. It will not be denied, that power is of an encroaching nature, and that it ought to be effectually restrained from passing the limits assigned to it. After discriminating therefore in theory, the several classes of power, as they may in their nature be legislative, executive, or judiciary; the next and most difficult task, is to provide some practical security for each against the invasion of the others. What this security ought to be, is the great problem to be solved.

Will it be sufficient to mark with precision the boundaries of these departments in the Constitution of the government, and to trust to these parchment barriers against the encroaching spirit of power? This is the security which appears to have been principally relied on by the compilers of most of the American Constitutions. But experience assures us, that the efficacy of the provision has been greatly over-rated; and that some more adequate defence is indispensibly necessary for the more feeble, against the more powerful members of the government. The legislative department is every where extending the sphere of its activity, and drawing all power into its impetuous vortex.

The founders of our republics have so much merit for the wisdom which they have displayed, that no task can be less pleasing than that of pointing out the errors into which they have fallen. A respect for truth however obliges us to remark, that they seem never for a moment to have turned their eyes from the danger to liberty from the overgrown and all-grasping prerogative of an hereditary magistrate, supported and fortified by an hereditary branch of the legislative authority. They seem never to have recollected the danger from legislative usurpations; which by assembling all power in the same hands, must lead to the same tyranny as is threatened by executive usurpations.

In a government, where numerous and extensive prerogatives are placed in the hands of a hereditary monarch, the executive department is very justly regarded as the source of danger, and watched with all the jealousy which a zeal for liberty ought to inspire. In a democracy, where a multitude of people exercise in person the legislative functions, and are continually exposed by their incapacity for regular deliberation and concerted measures, to the ambitious intrigues of their executive magistrates, tyranny may well be apprehended on some favorable emergency, to start up in the same quarter. But in a representative republic, where the executive magistracy is carefully limited both in the extent and the duration of its power; and where the legislative power is exercised by an assembly, which is inspired by a supposed influence over the people with an intrepid confidence in its own strength; which is sufficiently numerous to feel all the passions which actuate a multitude; yet not so numerous as to be incapable of pursuing the objects of its passions, by means which reason prescribes; it is against the enterprising ambition of this department, that the people ought to indulge all their jealousy and exhaust all their precautions.

The legislative department derives a superiority in our governments from other circumstances. Its constitutional powers being at once more extensive and less susceptible of precise limits, it can with the greater facility, mask under complicated and indirect measures, the encroachments which it makes on the co-ordinate departments. It is not unfrequently a question of real-nicety in legislative bodies, whether the operation of a particular measure, will, or will not extend beyond the legislative sphere. On the other side, the executive power being restrained within a narrower compass, and being more simple in its nature; and the judiciary being described by land marks, still less uncertain, projects of usurpation by either of these departments, would immediately betray and defeat themselves. Nor is this all: As the legislative department alone has access to the pockets of the people, and has in some Constitutions full discretion, and in all, a prevailing influence over the pecuniary rewards of those who fill the other departments, a dependence is thus created in the latter, which gives still greater facility to encroachments of the former.

I have appealed to our own experience for the truth of what I advance on this subject. Were it necessary to verify this experience by particular proofs, they might be multiplied without end. I might find a witness in every citizen who has shared in, or been attentive to, the course of public administrations. I might collect vouchers in abundance from the records and archieves of every State in the Union. But as a more concise and at the same time, equally satisfactory evidence, I will refer to the example of two States, attested by two unexceptionable authorities.

The first example is that of Virginia, a State which, as we have seen, has expressly declared in its Constitution, that the three great departments ought not to be intermixed. The authority in support of it is Mr. Jefferson, who, besides his other advantages for remarking the operation of the government, was himself the chief magistrate of it. In order to convey fully the ideas with which his experience had impressed him on this subject, it will be necessary to quote a passage of some length from his very interesting "Notes on the State of Virginia." (P. 195.) "All the powers of government, legislative, executive and judiciary, result to the legislative body. The concentrating these in the same hands is precisely the definition of despotic government. It will be no alleviation that these powers will be exercised by a plurality of hands, and not by a single one, 173 despots would surely be as oppressive as one. Let those who doubt it turn their eyes on the republic of Venice. As little will it avail us that they are chosen by ourselves. An *elective despotism*, was not the government we fought for; but one which should not only be founded on free principles, but in which the powers of government should be so divided and balanced among several bodies of magistracy, as that no one could transcend their legal limits, without being effectually checked and restrained by the others. For this reason that Convention which passed the ordinance of government, laid its foundation on this basis, that the legislative, executive and judiciary departments should be separate and distinct, so that no person should exercise the powers of more than one of them at the same time. *But no barrier was provided between these several powers.* The judiciary and executive members were left dependent on the legislative for their subsistence in office, and some of them for their continuance in it. If therefore the Legislature assumes executive and judiciary powers, no opposition is likely to be made; nor if made can it be effectual; because in that case, they may put their proceeding into the form of an act of Assembly, which will render them obligatory on the other branches. They have accordingly *in many* instances *decided rights* which should have been left to *judiciary controversy*; and *the direction of the executive during the whole time of their session, is becoming habitual and familiar."*

The other State, which I shall take for an example, is Pennsylvania; and the other authority the council of censors which assembled in the years 1783 and 1784. A part of the duty of this body, as marked out by the Constitution was, "to enquire whether the Constitution had been preserved inviolate in every part; and whether the legislative and executive branches of government had performed their duty as guardians of the people, or assumed to themselves, or exercised other or greater powers than they are entitled to by the Constitution." In the execution of this trust, the council were necessarily led to a comparison, of both the legislative and executive proceedings, with the constitutional powers of these departments; and from the facts enumerated, and to the truth of most of which, both sides in the council subscribed, it appears that the Constitution had been flagrantly violated by the Legislature in a variety of important instances.

A great number of laws had been passed violating without any apparent necessity, the rule requiring that all bills of a public nature, shall be previously printed for the consideration of the people; altho' this is one of the precautions chiefly relied on by the Constitution, against improper acts of the Legislature.

The constitutional trial by jury had been violated; and powers assumed, which had not been delegated by the Constitution.

Executive powers had been usurped.

The salaries of the Judges, which the Constitution expressly requires to be fixed, had been occasionally varied; and cases belonging to the judiciary department, frequently drawn within legislative cognizance and determination.

Those who wish to see the several particulars falling under each of these heads, may consult the Journals of the council which are in print. Some of them, it will be found may be imputable to peculiar circumstances connected with the war: But the greater part of them may be considered as the spontaneous shoots of an ill-constituted government.

It appears also, that the executive had not been innocent of frequent breaches of the Constitution. There are three observations however, which ought to be made on this head. *First.* A great proportion of the instances, were either immediately produced by the necessities of the war, or recommended by Congress or the Commander in Chief. *Secondly.* In most of the other instances, they conformed either to the declared or the known sentiments of the legislative department. *Thirdly.* The executive department of Pennsylvania is distinguished from that of the other States, by the number of members composing it. In this respect it has as much affinity to a legislative assembly, as to an executive council. And being at once exempt from the restraint of an individual responsibility for the acts of the body, and deriving confidence from mutual example and joint influence; unauthorized measures would of course be more freely hazarded, than where the executive department is administered by a single hand or by a few hands.

The conclusion which I am warranted in drawing from these observations is, that a mere demarkation on parchment of the constitutional limits of the several departments, is not a sufficient guard against those encroachments which lead to a tyrannical concentration of all the powers of government in the same hands.

PUBLIUS.

THE FEDERALIST NO. 51

JAMES MADISON

FEBRUARY 6, 1788

To the People of the State of New York.

To what expedient then shall we finally resort for maintaining in practice the necessary partition of power among the several departments, as laid down in the constitution? The only answer that can be given is, that as all these exterior provisions are found to be inadequate, the defect must be supplied, by so contriving the interior structure of the government, as that its several constituent parts may, by their mutual relations, be the means of keeping each other in their proper places. Without presuming to undertake a full developement of this important idea, I will hazard a few general observations, which may perhaps place it in a clearer light, and enable us to form a more correct judgment of the principles and structure of the government planned by the convention.

In order to lay a due foundation for that separate and distinct exercise of the different powers of government, which to a certain extent, is admitted on all hands to be essential to the preservation of liberty, it is evident that each department should have a will of its own; and consequently should be so constituted, that the members of each should have as little agency as possible in the appointment of the members of the others. Were this principle rigorously adhered to, it would require that all the appointments for the supreme executive, legislative, and judiciary magistracies, should be drawn from the same fountain of authority, the people, through channels, having no communication whatever with one another. Perhaps such a plan of constructing the several departments would be less difficult in practice than it may in contemplation appear. Some difficulties however, and some additional expence, would attend the execution of it. Some deviations therefore from the principle must be admitted. In the constitution of the judiciary department in particular, it might be inexpedient to insist rigorously on the principle; first, because peculiar qualifications being essential in the members, the primary consideration ought to be to select that mode of choice, which best secures these qualifications; secondly, because the permanent tenure by which the appointments are held in that department, must soon destroy all sense of dependence on the authority conferring them.

It is equally evident that the members of each department should be as little dependent as possible on those of the others, for the emoluments annexed to their offices. Were the executive magistrate, or the judges, not independent of the legislature in this particular, their independence in every other would be merely nominal.

But the great security against a gradual concentration of the several powers in the same department, consists in giving to those who administer each department, the necessary constitutional means, and personal motives, to resist encroachments of the others. The provision for defence must in this, as in all other cases, be made commensurate to the danger of attack. Ambition must be made to counteract ambition.

The interest of the man must be connected with the constitutional rights of the place. It may be a reflection on human nature, that such devices should be necessary to controul the abuses of government. But what is government itself but the greatest of all reflections on human nature? If men were angels, no government would be necessary. If angels were to govern men, neither external nor internal controuls on government would be necessary. In framing a government which is to be administered by men over men, the great difficulty lies in this: You must first enable the government to controul the governed; and in the next place, oblige it to controul itself. A dependence on the people is no doubt the primary controul on the government; but experience has taught mankind the necessity of auxiliary precautions.

This policy of supplying by opposite and rival interests, the defect of better motives, might be traced through the whole system of human affairs, private as well as public. We see it particularly displayed in all the subordinate distributions of power; where the constant aim is to divide and arrange the several offices in such a manner as that each may be a check on the other; that the private interest of every individual, may be a centinel over the public rights. These inventions of prudence cannot be less requisite in the distribution of the supreme powers of the state.

But it is not possible to give to each department an equal power of self defence. In republican government the legislative authority, necessarily, predominates. The remedy for this inconveniency is, to divide the legislature into different branches; and to render them by different modes of election, and different principles of action, as little connected with each other, as the nature of their common functions, and their common dependence on the society, will admit. It may even be necessary to guard against dangerous encroachments by still further precautions. As the weight of the legislative authority requires that it should be thus divided, the weakness of the executive may require, on the other hand, that it should be fortified. An absolute negative, on the legislature, appears at first view to be the natural defence with which the executive magistrate should be armed. But perhaps it would be neither altogether safe, nor alone sufficient. On ordinary occasions, it might not be exerted with the requisite firmness; and on extraordinary occasions, it might be perfidiously abused. May not this defect of an absolute negative be supplied, by some qualified connection between this weaker department, and the weaker branch of the stronger department, by which the latter may be led to support the constitutional rights of the former, without being too much detached from the rights of its own department?

If the principles on which these observations are founded be just, as I persuade myself they are, and they be applied as a criterion, to the several state constitutions, and to the federal constitution, it will be found, that if the latter does not perfectly correspond with them, the former are infinitely less able to bear such a test.

There are moreover two considerations particularly applicable to the federal system of America, which place that system in a very interesting point of view.

First. In a single republic, all the power surrendered by the people, is submitted to the administration of a single government; and usurpations are guarded against by a division of the government into distinct and separate departments. In the compound republic of America, the power surrendered by the people, is first divided between two distinct governments, and then the portion allotted to each, subdivided among distinct and separate departments. Hence a double security arises to the rights of the people. The different governments will controul each other; at the same time that each will be controuled by itself.

Second. It is of great importance in a republic, not only to guard the society against the oppression of its rulers; but to guard one part of the society against the injustice of the other part. Different interests necessarily exist in different classes of citizens. If a majority be united by a common interest, the rights of the minority will be insecure. There are but two methods of providing against this evil: The one by creating a will in the community independent of the majority, that is of the society itself; the other by comprehending in the society so many separate descriptions of citizens, as will render an unjust combination of a majority of the whole, very improbable, if not impracticable. The first method prevails in all governments possessing an hereditary or self appointed authority. This at best is but a precarious security; because a power independent of the society may as well espouse the unjust views of the major, as the rightful interests, of the minor party, and may possibly be turned against both parties. The second method will be exemplified in the federal republic of the United States. Whilst all authority in it will be derived from and dependent on the society, the society itself will be broken into so many parts, interests and

classes of citizens, that the rights of individuals or of
the minority, will be in little danger from interested
combinations of the majority. In a free government,
the security for civil rights must be the same as for religious rights. It consists in the one case in the multiplicity of interests, and in the other, in the multiplicity
of sects. The degree of security in both cases will depend on the number of interests and sects; and this
may be presumed to depend on the extent of country
and number of people comprehended under the same
government. This view of the subject must particularly
recommend a proper federal system to all the sincere
and considerate friends of republican government:
Since it shews that in exact proportion as the territory
of the union may be formed into more circumscribed
confederacies or states, oppressive combinations of a
majority will be facilitated, the best security under the
republican form, for the rights of every class of citizens,
will be diminished; and consequently, the stability and
independence of some member of the government, the
only other security, must be proportionally increased.
Justice is the end of government. It is the end of civil
society. It ever has been, and ever will be pursued, until
it be obtained, or until liberty be lost in the pursuit. In
a society under the forms of which the stronger faction
can readily unite and oppress the weaker, anarchy may
as truly be said to reign, as in a state of nature where
the weaker individual is not secured against the violence of the stronger: And as in the latter state even the
stronger individuals are prompted by the uncertainty
of their condition, to submit to a government which
may protect the weak as well as themselves: So in the
former state, will the more powerful factions or parties

be gradually induced by a like motive, to wish for a government which will protect all parties, the weaker as well as the more powerful. It can be little doubted, that if the state of Rhode Island was separated from the confederacy, and left to itself, the insecurity of rights under the popular form of government within such narrow limits, would be displayed by such reiterated oppressions of factious majorities, that some power altogether independent of the people would soon be called for by the voice of the very factions whose misrule had proved the necessity of it. In the extended republic of the United States, and among the great variety of interests, parties and sects which it embraces, a coalition of a majority of the whole society could seldom take place on any other principles than those of justice and the general good; and there being thus less danger to a minor from the will of the major party, there must be less pretext also, to provide for the security of the former, by introducing into the government a will not dependent on the latter; or in other words, a will independent of the society itself. It is no less certain than it is important, notwithstanding the contrary opinions which have been entertained, that the larger the society, provided it lie within a practicable sphere, the more duly capable it will be of self government. And happily for the *republican cause*, the practicable sphere may be carried to a very great extent, by a judicious modification and mixture of the *federal principle*.

PUBLIUS.

THE FEDERALIST NO. 62

JAMES MADISON

FEBRUARY 27, 1788

To the People of the State of New York.

Having examined the constitution of the house of representatives, and answered such of the objections against it as seemed to merit notice, I enter next on the examination of the senate. The heads into which this member of the government may be considered, are I. the qualifications of senators. II. the appointment of them by the state legislatures. III. the equality of representation in the senate. IV. the number of senators, and the term for which they are to be elected. V. the powers vested in the senate.

I. The qualifications proposed for senators, as distinguished from those of representatives, consist in a more advanced age, and a longer period of citizenship. A senator must be thirty years of age at least; as a representative, must be twenty-five. And the former must have been a citizen nine years; as seven years are required for the latter. The propriety of these distinctions is explained by the nature of the senatorial trust; which requiring greater extent of information and stability of character, requires at the same time that the senator should have reached a period of life most likely to supply these advantages; and which participating immediately in transactions with foreign nations, ought to be exercised by none who are not thoroughly weaned from the prepossessions and habits incident to foreign birth and education. The term of nine years appears to be a prudent mediocrity between a total exclusion of adopted citizens, whose merit and talents may claim a share in the public confidence; and an indiscriminate and hasty admission of them, which might create a channel for foreign influence on the national councils.

II. It is equally unnecessary to dilate on the appointment of senators by the state legislatures. Among the various modes which might have been devised for constituting this branch of the government, that which has been proposed by the convention is probably the most congenial with the public opinion. It is recommended by the double advantage of favouring a select appointment, and of giving to the state governments such an agency in the formation of the federal government, as must secure the authority of the former; and may form a convenient link between the two systems.

III. The equality of representation in the senate is another point, which, being evidently the result of compromise between the opposite pretensions of the large and the small states, does not call for much discussion. If indeed it be right that among a people thoroughly incorporated into one nation, every district ought to have a *proportional* share in the government; and that among independent and sovereign states bound together by a simple league, the parties however unequal in size, ought to have an *equal* share in the common councils, it does not appear to be without some reason, that in a compound republic partaking both of the national and federal character, the government ought to be founded on a mixture of the principles of proportional and equal representation. But it is superfluous to try by the standards of theory, a part of the constitution which is allowed on all hands to be the result not of theory, but "of a spirit of amity, and that mutual deference and concession which the peculiarity of our political situation rendered indispensable." A common government with powers equal to its objects, is called for by the voice, and still more loudly by the political situation of America. A government founded on principles more consonant to the wishes of the larger states, is not likely to be obtained from the smaller states. The only option then for the former lies between the proposed government and a government still more objectionable. Under this alternative the advice of prudence must be, to embrace the lesser evil; and instead of indulging a fruitless anticipation of the possible mischiefs which may ensue, to contemplate rather the advantageous consequences which may qualify the sacrifice.

In this spirit it may be remarked, that the equal vote allowed to each state, is at once a constitutional recognition of the portion of sovereignty remaining in the individual states, and an instrument for preserving that residuary sovereignty. So far the equality ought to be no less acceptable to the large than to the small states; since they are not less solicitous to guard by every possible expedient against an improper consolidation of the states into one simple republic.

Another advantage accruing from this ingredient in the constitution of the senate, is the additional impediment it must prove against improper acts of legislation. No law or resolution can now be passed without the concurrence first of a majority of the people, and then of a majority of the states. It must be acknowledged that this complicated check on legislation may in some instances be injurious as well as beneficial; and that the peculiar defence which it involves in favour of the smaller states would be more rational, if any interests common to them, and distinct from those of the other states, would otherwise be exposed to peculiar danger. But as the larger states will always be able by their power over the supplies to defeat unreasonable exertions of this prerogative of the lesser states; and as the facility and excess of law-making seem to be the diseases to which our governments are most liable, it is not impossible that this part of the constitution may be more convenient in practice than it appears to many in contemplation.

IV. The number of senators and the duration of their appointment come next to be considered. In order to form an accurate judgment on both these points, it will be proper to enquire into the purposes which are to be answered by a senate; and in order to ascertain these it will be necessary to review the inconveniencies which a republic must suffer from the want of such an institution.

First. It is a misfortune incident to republican government, though in a less degree than to other governments, that those who administer it, may forget their obligations to their constituents, and prove unfaithful to their important trust. In this point of view, a senate, as a second branch of the legislative assembly, distinct from, and dividing the power with, a first, must be in all cases a salutary check on the government. It doubles the security to the people, by requiring the concurrence of two distinct bodies in schemes of usurpation or perfidy, where the ambition or corruption of one, would otherwise be sufficient. This is a precaution founded on such clear principles, and now so well understood in the United States, that it would be more than superfluous to enlarge on it. I will barely remark that as the improbability of sinister combinations will be in proportion to the dissimilarity in the genius of the two bodies; it must be politic to distinguish them from each other by every circumstance which will consist with a due harmony in all proper measures, and with the genuine principles of republican government.

Secondly. The necessity of a senate is not less indicated by the propensity of all single and numerous assemblies, to yield to the impulse of sudden and violent passions, and to be seduced by factious leaders, into intemperate and pernicious resolutions. Examples on this subject might be cited without number; and from proceedings within the United States, as well as from the history of other nations. But a position that will not be contradicted need not be proved. All that need be remarked is that a body which is to correct this infirmity ought itself be free from it, and consequently ought to be less numerous. It ought moreover to possess great firmness, and consequently ought to hold its authority by a tenure of considerable duration.

Thirdly. Another defect to be supplied by a senate lies in a want of due acquaintance with the objects and principles of legislation. It is not possible that an assembly of men called for the most part from pursuits of a private nature, continued in appointment for a short time, and led by no permanent motive to devote the intervals of public occupation to a study of the laws, the affairs and the comprehensive interests of their country, should, if left wholly to themselves, escape a variety of important errors in the exercise of their legislative trust. It may be affirmed, on the best grounds, that no small share of the present embarrassments of America is to be charged on the blunders of our governments; and that these have proceeded from the heads rather than the hearts of most of the authors of them. What indeed are all the repealing, explaining and amending laws, which fill and disgrace our voluminous codes, but so many monuments of deficient wisdom; so many impeachments exhibited by each succeeding, against each preceding session; so many admonitions to the people of the value of those aids which may be expected from a well constituted senate?

A good government implies two things; first, fidelity to the object of government, which is the happiness of the people; secondly, a knowledge of the means by which that object can be best attained. Some governments are deficient in both these qualities: Most governments are deficient in the first. I scruple not to assert that in the American governments, too little attention has been paid to the last. The federal constitution avoids this error; and what merits particular notice, it provides for the last in a mode which increases the security for the first.

Fourthly. The mutability in the public councils, arising from a rapid succession of new members, however qualified they may be, points out in the strongest manner, the necessity of some stable institution in the government. Every new election in the states, is found to change one half of the representatives. From this change of men must proceed a change of opinions; and from a change of opinions, a change of measures. But a continual change even of good measures is inconsistent with every rule of prudence, and every prospect of success. The remark is verified in private life, and becomes more just as well as more important, in national transactions.

To trace the mischievous effects of a mutable government would fill a volume. I will hint a few only, each of which will be perceived to be a source of innumerable others.

In the first place it forfeits the respect and confidence of other nations, and all the advantages connected with national character. An individual who is observed to be inconstant to his plans, or perhaps to carry on his affairs without any plan at all, is marked at once by all prudent people as a speedy victim to his own unsteadiness and folly. His more friendly neighbours may pity him; but all will decline to connect their fortunes with his; and not a few will seize the opportunity of making their fortunes out of his. One nation is to another what one individual is to another; with this melancholy distinction perhaps, that the former with fewer of the benevolent emotions than the latter, are under fewer restraints also from taking undue advantage of the indiscretions of each other. Every nation consequently whose affairs betray a want of wisdom and stability, may calculate on every loss which can be sustained from the more systematic policy of its wiser neighbours. But the best instruction on this subject is unhappily conveyed to America by the example of her own situation. She finds that she is held in no respect by her friends; that she is the derision of her enemies; and that she is a prey to every nation which has an interest in speculating on her fluctuating councils and embarrassed affairs.

The internal effects of a mutable policy are still

more calamitous. It poisons the blessings of liberty it-self. It will be of little avail to the people that the laws are made by men of their own choice, if the laws be so voluminous that they cannot be read, or so incoherent that they cannot be understood; if they be repealed or revised before they are promulged, or undergo such incessant changes that no man who knows what the law is to-day can guess what it will be to-morrow. Law is defined to be a rule of action; but how can that be a rule, which is little known and less fixed?

Another effect of public instability is the unreason-able advantage it gives to the sagacious, the enterpris-ing and the moneyed few, over the industrious and uninformed mass of the people. Every new regulation concerning commerce or revenue, or in any manner affecting the value of the different species of property, presents a new harvest to those who watch the change, and can trace its consequences; a harvest reared not by themselves but by the toils and cares of the great body of their fellow citizens. This is a state of things in which it may be said with some truth that laws are made for the *few* not for the *many*.

In another point of view great injury results from an unstable government. The want of confidence in the public councils damps every useful undertaking; the success and profit of which may depend on a continu-ance of existing arrangements. What prudent mer-chant will hazard his fortunes in any new branch of commerce, when he knows not but that his plans may be rendered unlawful before they can be executed? What farmer or manufacturer will lay himself out for the encouragement given to any particular cultivation or establishment, when he can have no assurance that his preparatory labors and advances will not render him a victim to an inconstant government? In a word no great improvement or laudable enterprise, can go forward, which requires the auspices of a steady system of national policy.

But the most deplorable effect of all is that diminution of attachment and reverence which steals into the hearts of the people, towards a political system which betrays so many marks of infirmity, and disappoints so many of their flattering hopes. No government any more than an individual will long be respected, without being truly respectable, nor be truly respectable without possessing a certain portion of order and stability.

PUBLIUS.

THE FEDERALIST NO. 63

JAMES MADISON

MARCH 1, 1788

To the People of the State of New York.

A FIFTH desideratum illustrating the utility of a Senate, is the want of a due sense of national character. Without a select and stable member of the government, the esteem of foreign powers will not only be forfeited by an unenlightened and variable policy, proceeding from the causes already mentioned; but the national councils will not possess that sensibility to the opinion of the world, which is perhaps not less necessary in order to merit, than it is to obtain, its respect and confidence.

An attention to the judgment of other nations is important to every government for two reasons: The one is, that independently of the merits of any particular plan or measure, it is desireable on various accounts, that it should appear to other nations as the offspring of a wise and honorable policy: The second is, that in doubtful cases, particularly where the national councils may be warped by some strong passion, or momentary interest, the presumed or known opinion of the impartial world, may be the best guide that can be followed. What has not America lost by her want of character with foreign nations? And how many errors and follies would she not have avoided, if the justice and propriety of her measures had in every instance been previously tried by the light in which they would probably appear to the unbiassed part of mankind?

Yet however requisite a sense of national character may be, it is evident that it can never be sufficiently possessed by a numerous and changeable body. It can only be found in a number so small, that a sensible degree of the praise and blame of public measures may be the portion of each individual; or in an assembly so durably invested with public trust, that the pride and consequence of its members may be sensibly incorporated with the reputation and prosperity of the community. The half-yearly representatives of Rhode-Island, would probably have been little affected in their deliberations on the iniquitous measures of that state, by arguments drawn from the light in which such measures would be viewed by foreign nations, or even by the sister states; whilst it can scarcely be doubted, that if the concurrence of a select and stable body had been necessary, a regard to national character alone, would have prevented the calamities under which that misguided people is now labouring.

I add as a *sixth* defect, the want in some important cases of a due responsibility in the government to the people, arising from that frequency of elections, which in other cases produces this responsibility. This remark will perhaps appear not only new but paradoxical. It must nevertheless be acknowledged, when explained, to be as undeniable as it is important.

Responsibility in order to be reasonable must be limited to objects within the power of the responsible party; and in order to be effectual, must relate to operations of that power, of which a ready and proper judgment can be formed by the constituents. The objects of government may be divided into two general classes; the one depending on measures which have singly an immediate and sensible operation; the other depending on a succession of well chosen and well connected measures, which have a gradual and perhaps unobserved operation. The importance of the latter description to the collective and permanent welfare of every country needs no explanation. And yet it is evident, that an assembly elected for so short a term as to be unable to provide more than one or two links in a chain of measures, on which the general welfare may essentially depend, ought not to be answerable for the final result, any more than a steward or tenant, engaged for one year, could be justly made to answer for places or improvements, which could not be accomplished in less than half a dozen years. Nor is it possible for the people to estimate the *share* of influence which their annual assemblies may respectively have on events resulting from the mixed transactions of several years. It is sufficiently difficult at any rate to preserve a personal responsibility in the members of a *numerous* body, for such acts of the body as have an immediate, detached and palpable operation on its constituents.

The proper remedy for this defect must be an additional body in the legislative department, which, having sufficient permanency to provide for such objects as require a continued attention, and a train of measures, may be justly and effectually answerable for the attainment of those objects.

Thus far I have considered the circumstances which point out the necessity of a well constructed senate, only as they relate to the representatives of the people. To a people as little blinded by prejudice, or corrupted by flattery, as those whom I address, I shall not scruple to add, that such an institution may be sometimes necessary, as a defence to the people against their own temporary errors and delusions. As the cool and deliberate sense of the community ought in all governments, and actually will in all free governments ultimately prevail over the views of its rulers; so there are particular moments in public affairs, when the people stimulated by some irregular passion, or some illicit advantage, or misled by the artful misrepresentations of interested men, may call for measures which they themselves will afterwards be the most ready to lament and condemn. In these critical moments, how salutary will be the interference of some temperate and respectable body of citizens, in order to check the misguided career, and to suspend the blow meditated by the people against themselves, until reason, justice and truth, can regain their authority over the public mind? What bitter anguish would not the people of Athens have often escaped, if their government had contained so provident a safeguard against the tyranny of their own passions? Popular liberty might then have escaped the indelible reproach of decreeing to the same citizens, the hemlock on one day, and statues on the next.

It may be suggested that a people spread over an extensive region, cannot like the crouded inhabitants of a small district, be subject to the infection of violent passions; or to the danger of combining in the pursuit of unjust measures. I am far from denying that this is a distinction of peculiar importance. I have on the contrary endeavoured in a former paper, to shew that it is one of the principal recommendations of a confederated republic. At the same time this advantage ought not to be considered as superseding the use of auxiliary precautions. It may even be remarked that the same extended situation which will exempt the people of America from some of the dangers incident to lesser republics, will expose them to the inconveniency of remaining for a longer time, under the influence of those misrepresentations which the combined industry of interested men may succeed in distributing among them.

It adds no small weight to all these considerations, to recollect, that history informs us of no long lived republic which had not a senate. Sparta, Rome and Carthage are in fact the only states to whom that character can be applied. In each of the two first there was a senate for life. The constitution of the senate in the last, is less known. Circumstantial evidence makes it probable that it was not different in this particular from the two others. It is at least certain that it had some quality or other which rendered it an anchor against popular fluctuations; and that a smaller council drawn out of the senate was appointed not only for life; but filled up vacancies itself. These examples, though as unfit for the imitation, as they are repugnant to the genius of America, are notwithstanding, when compared with the fugitive and turbulent existence of other antient republics, very instructive proofs of the necessity of some institution that will blend stability with liberty. I am not unaware of the circumstances which distinguish the American from other popular governments, as well antient as modern; and which render extreme circumspection necessary in reasoning from the one case to the other. But after allowing due weight to this consideration, it may still be maintained that there are many points of similitude which render these examples not unworthy of our attention. Many of the defects as we have seen, which can only be supplied by a senatorial institution, are common to a numerous assembly frequently elected by the people, and to the people themselves. There are others peculiar to the former, which require the controul of such an institution. The people can never wilfully betray their own interests: But they may possibly be betrayed by the representatives of the people; and the danger will be evidently greater where the whole legislative trust is lodged in the hands of one body of men, than where the concurrence of separate and dissimilar bodies is required in every public act.

The difference most relied on between the American and other republics, consists in the principle of representation, which is the pivot on which the former move, and which is supposed to have been unknown to the latter, or at least to the antient part of them. The use which has been made of this difference, in reasonings contained in former papers, will have shewn that I am disposed neither to deny its existence nor to undervalue its importance. I feel the less restraint therefore in observing that the position concerning the ignorance of the antient government on the subject of representation is by no means precisely true in the latitude commonly given to it. Without entering into a disquisition which here would be misplaced, I will refer to a few known facts in support of what I advance.

In the most pure democracies of Greece, many of the executive functions were performed not by the people themselves, but by officers elected by the people, and *representing* the people in their *executive* capacity.

Prior to the reform of Solon, Athens was governed by nine Archons, annually *elected by the people at large*. The degree of power delegated to them seems to be left in great obscurity. Subsequent to that period, we find an assembly first of four and afterwards of six hundred members, annually *elected by the people*; and *partially* representing them in their *legislative* capacity; since they were not only associated with the people in the function of making laws; but had the exclusive right of originating legislative propositions to the people. The senate of Carthage also, whatever might be its power or the duration of its appointment, appears to have been *elective* by the suffrages of the people. Similar instances might be traced in most if not all the popular governments of antiquity.

Lastly in Sparta, we meet with the Ephori, and in

Rome with the Tribunes; two bodies, small indeed in number, but annually *elected by the whole body of the people*, and considered as the *representatives* of the people, almost in their *plenipotentiary* capacity. The Cosmi of Crete were also annually *elected by the people*; and have been considered by some authors as an institution analogous to those of Sparta and Rome; with this difference only that in the election of that representative body, the right of suffrage was communicated to a part only of the people.

From these facts, to which many others might be added, it is clear that the principle of representation was neither unknown to the antients, nor wholly overlooked in their political constitutions. The true distinction between these and the American Governments lies *in the total exclusion of the people in their collective capacity* from any share in the *latter*, and not in the *total exclusion of representatives of the people*, from the administration of the *former*. The distinction however thus qualified must be admitted to leave a most advantageous superiority in favor of the United States. But to ensure to this advantage its full effect, we must be careful not to separate it from the other advantage, of an extensive territory. For it cannot be believed that any form of representative government, could have succeeded within the narrow limits occupied by the democracies of Greece.

In answer to all these arguments, suggested by reason, illustrated by examples, and enforced by our own experience, the jealous adversary of the constitution will probably content himself with repeating, that a senate appointed not immediately by the people, and for the term of six years, must gradually acquire a dangerous preeminence in the government, and finally transform it into a tyrannical aristocracy.

To this general answer the general reply ought to be sufficient; that liberty may be endangered by the abuses of liberty, as well as by the abuses of power; that there are numerous instances of the former as well as of the latter; and that the former rather than the latter is apparently most to be apprehended by the United States. But a more particular reply may be given.

Before such a revolution can be effected, the senate, it is to be observed, must in the first place corrupt itself; must next corrupt the state legislatures, must then corrupt the house of representatives, and must finally corrupt the people at large. It is evident that the senate must be first corrupted, before it can attempt an establishment of tyranny. Without corrupting the state legislatures, it cannot prosecute the attempt, because the periodical change of members would otherwise regenerate the whole body. Without exerting the means of corruption with equal success on the house of representatives, the opposition of that co-equal branch of the government would inevitably defeat the attempt; and without corrupting the people themselves, a succession of new representatives would speedily restore all things to their pristine order. Is there any man who can seriously persuade himself, that the proposed senate can, by any possible means within the compass of human address, arrive at the object of a lawless ambition, through all these obstructions?

If reason condemns the suspicion, the same sentence is pronounced by experience. The constitution of Maryland furnishes the most apposite example. The senate of that state is elected, as the federal senate will be, indirectly by the people; and for a term less by one year only, than the federal senate. It is distinguished also by the remarkable prerogative of filling up its own vacancies within the term of its appointment: and at the same time, is not under the controul of any such rotation, as is provided for the federal senate. There are some other lesser distinctions, which would expose the former to colorable objections that do not lie against the latter. If the federal senate therefore really contained the danger which has been so loudly proclaimed, some symptoms at least of a like danger ought by this time to have been betrayed by the senate of Maryland; but no such symptoms have appeared. On the contrary the jealousies at first entertained by men of the same description with those who view with terror the correspondent part of the federal constitution, have been gradually extinguished by the progress of the experiment; and the Maryland constitution is daily deriving from the salutary operations of this part of it, a reputation in which it will probably not be rivalled by that of any state in the union.

But if any thing could silence the jealousies on this subject, it ought to be the British example. The senate there, instead of being elected for a term of six years, and of being unconfined to particular families or fortunes, is an hereditary assembly of opulent nobles. The house of representatives, instead of being elected for two years and by the whole body of the people, is elected for seven years; and in very great proportion, by a very small proportion of the people. Here unquestionably ought to be seen in full display, the aristocratic usurpations and tyranny, which are at some future period to be exemplified in the United States. Unfortunately however for the antifederal argument the British history informs us, that this hereditary assembly has not even been able to defend itself against the continual encroachments of the house of representatives; and that it no sooner lost the support of the monarch, than it was actually crushed by the weight of the popular branch.

As far as antiquity can instruct us on this subject, its examples support the reasoning which we have employed. In Sparta the Ephori, the annual representatives of the people, were found an overmatch for the senate for life, continually gained on its authority, and finally drew all power into their own hands. The tribunes of Rome, who were the representatives of the people, prevailed, it is well known, in almost every contest with the senate for life, and in the end gained the most complete triumph over it. This fact is the more remarkable, as unanimity was required in every act of the tribunes, even after their number was augmented to ten. It proves the irresistable force possessed by that branch of a free government, which has the people on its side. To these examples might be added that of Carthage, whose senate, according to the testimony of Polybius, instead of drawing all power into its vortex, had at the commencement of the second punic war, lost almost the whole of its original portion.

Besides the conclusive evidence resulting from this assemblage of facts, that the federal senate will never be able to transform itself, by gradual usurpations, into an independent and aristocratic body; we are warranted in believing that if such a revolution should ever happen from causes which the foresight of man cannot guard against, the house of representatives with the people on their side will at all times be able to bring back the constitution to its primitive form and principles. Against the force of the immediate representatives of the people, nothing will be able to maintain even the constitutional authority of the senate, but such a display of enlightened policy, and attachment to the public good, as will divide with that branch of the legislature, the affections and support of the entire body of the people themselves.

PUBLIUS.

THE FEDERALIST NO. 64

JOHN JAY

MARCH 5, 1788

To the People of the State of New York.

It is a just and not a new observation, that enemies to particular persons and opponents to particular measures, seldom confine their censures to such things only in either, as are worthy of blame. Unless on this principle it is difficult to explain the motives of their conduct, who condemn the proposed constitution in the aggregate, and treat with severity some of the most unexceptionable articles in it.

The 2d. section gives power to the president "*by and with the advice and consent of the senate to make treaties* PROVIDED TWO THIRDS OF THE SENATORS PRESENT CONCUR."

The power of making treaties is an important one,

especially as it relates to war, peace and commerce; and it should not be delegated but in such a mode, and with such precautions, as will afford the highest security, that it will be exercised by men the best qualified for the purpose, and in the manner most conducive to the public good. The convention appears to have been attentive to both these points—they have directed the president to be chosen by select bodies of electors to be deputed by the people for that express purpose; and they have committed the appointment of senators to the state legislatures. This mode has in such cases, vastly the advantage of elections by the people in their collective capacity, where the activity of party zeal taking advantage of the supineness, the ignorance, and the hopes and fears of the unwary and interested, often places men in office by the votes of a small proportion of the electors.

As the select assemblies for choosing the president, as well as the state legislatures who appoint the senators will in general be composed of the most enlightened and respectable citizens, there is reason to presume that their attention and their votes will be directed to those men only who have become the most distinguished by their abilities and virtue, and in whom the people perceive just grounds for confidence. The constitution manifests very particular attention to this object. By excluding men under thirty five from the first office, and those under thirty from the second, it confines the electors to men of whom the people have had time to form a judgment, and with respect to whom they will not be liable to be deceived by those brilliant appearances of genius and patriotism, which like transient meteors sometimes mislead as well as dazzle. If the observation be well founded, that wise kings will always be served by able ministers, it is fair to argue that as an assembly of select electors possess in a greater degree than kings, the means of extensive and accurate information relative to men and characters, so will their appointments bear at least equal marks of discretion and discernment. The inference which naturally results from these considerations is this, that the president and senators so chosen will always be of the number of those who best understand our national interests, whether considered in relation to the several states or to foreign nations, who are best able to promote those interests, and whose reputation for integrity inspires and merits confidence. With such men the power of making treaties may be safely lodged.

Although the absolute necessity of system in the conduct of any business, is universally known and acknowledged, yet the high importance of it in national affairs has not yet become sufficiently impressed on the public mind. They who wish to commit the power under consideration to a popular assembly, composed of members constantly coming and going in quick succession, seem not to recollect that such a body must necessarily be inadequate to the attainment of those great objects, which require to be steadily contemplated in all their relations and circumstances, and which can only be approached and achieved by measures, which not only talents, but also exact information and often much time are necessary to concert and to execute. It was wise therefore in the convention to provide not only that the power of making treaties should be committed to able and honest men, but also that they should continue in place a sufficient time to become perfectly acquainted with our national concerns, and to form and introduce a system for the management of them. The duration prescribed is such as will give them an opportunity of greatly extending their political informations and of rendering their accumulating experience more and more beneficial to their country. Nor has the convention discovered less prudence in providing for the frequent elections of senators in such a way, as to obviate the inconvenience of periodically transferring those great affairs entirely to new men, for by leaving a considerable residue of the old ones in place, uniformity and order, as well as a constant succession of official information, will be preserved.

There are few who will not admit that the affairs of trade and navigation should be regulated by a system cautiously formed and steadily pursued; and that both our treaties and our laws should correspond with, and be made to promote it. It is of much consequence that this correspondence and conformity be carefully maintained, and they who assent to the truth of this position, will see and confess that it is well provided for by making the concurrence of the senate necessary both to treaties and to laws.

It seldom happens in the negociation of treaties of whatever nature, but that perfect *secrecy* and immediate *dispatch* are sometimes requisite. There are cases where the most useful intelligence may be obtained, if the persons possessing it can be relieved from apprehensions of discovery. Those apprehensions will operate on those persons whether they are actuated by mercenary or friendly motives, and there doubtless are many of both descriptions, who would rely on the secrecy of the president, but who would not confide in that of the senate, and still less in that of a large popular assembly. The convention have done well therefore in so disposing of the power of making treaties, that although the president must in forming them act by the advice and consent of the senate, yet he will be able to manage the business of intelligence in such manner as prudence may suggest.

They who have turned their attention to the affairs of men, must have perceived that there are tides in them. Tides, very irregular in their duration, strength and direction, and seldom found to run twice exactly in the same manner or measure. To discern and to profit by these tides in national affairs, is the business of those who preside over them; and they who have had much experience on this head inform us, that there frequently are occasions when days, nay even when hours are precious. The loss of a battle, the death of a Prince, the removal of a minister, or other circumstances intervening to change the present posture and aspect of affairs, may turn the most favorable tide into a course opposite to our wishes. As in the field, so in the cabinet, there are moments to be seized as they pass, and they who preside in either, should be left in capacity to improve them. So often and so essentially have we heretofore suffered from the want of secrecy and dispatch, that the Constitution would have been inexcusably defective if no attention had been paid to those objects. Those matters which in negociations usually require the most secrecy and the most dispatch, are those preparatory and auxiliary measures which are no otherwise important in a national view, than as they tend to facilitate the attainment of the objects of the negociation. For these the president will find no difficulty to provide, and should any circumstance occur which requires the advice and consent of the senate, he may at any time convene them. Thus we see that the constitution provides that our negociations for treaties shall have every advantage which can be derived from talents, information, integrity, and deliberate investigations on the one hand, and from secrecy and dispatch on the other.

But to this plan as to most others that have ever appeared, objections are contrived and urged.

Some are displeased with it, not on account of any errors or defects in it, but because as the treaties when made are to have the force of laws, they should be made only by men invested with legislative authority. These gentlemen seem not to consider that the judgments of our courts, and the commissions constitutionally given by our governor, are as valid and as binding on all persons whom they concern, as the laws passed by our legislature are. All constitutional acts of power, whether in the executive or in the judicial departments, have as much legal validity and obligation as if they proceeded from the Legislature, and therefore whatever name be given to the power of making treaties, or however obligatory they may be when made, certain it is that the people may with much propriety commit the power to a distinct body from the legislature, the executive or judicial. It surely does not follow that because they have given the power of making laws to the Legislature, that therefore they should likewise give them power to do every other act of sovereignty by which the citizens are to be bound and affected.

Others, though content that treaties should be made

in the mode proposed, are averse to their being the *supreme* laws of the land. They insist and profess to believe, that treaties, like acts of assembly, should be repealable at pleasure. This idea seems to be new and peculiar to this country, but new errors as well as new truths often appear. These gentlemen would do well to reflect that a treaty is only another name for a bargain; and that it would be impossible to find a nation who would make any bargain with us, which should be binding on them *absolutely*, but on us only so long and so far as we may think proper to be bound by it. They who make laws may without doubt amend or repeal them, and it will not be disputed that they who make treaties may alter or cancel them; but still let us not forget that treaties are made not by only one of the contracting parties, but by both, and consequently that as the consent of both was essential to their formation at first, so must it ever afterwards be to alter or cancel them. The proposed Constitution therefore has not in the least extended the obligation of treaties. They are just as binding, and just as far beyond the lawful reach of legislative acts now, as they will be at any future period, or under any form of government.

However useful jealousy may be in republics, yet when, like Bile in the natural, it abounds too much in the body politic; the eyes of both become very liable to be deceived by the delusive appearances which that malady casts on surrounding objects. From this cause probably proceed the fears and apprehensions of some, that the President and Senate may make treaties without an equal eye to the interests of all the States. Others suspect that the two-thirds will oppress the remaining

third, and ask whether those gentlemen are made sufficiently responsible for their conduct—whether if they
act corruptly they can be punished; and if they make
disadvantageous treaties, how are we to get rid of those
treaties?

As all the States are equally represented in the senate, and by men the most able and the most willing to
promote the interests of their constituents, they will all
have an equal degree of influence in that body, especially while they continue to be careful in appointing
proper persons, and to insist on their punctual attendance. In proportion as the United States assume a
national form, and a national character, so will the
good of the whole be more and more an object of attention; and the government must be a weak one indeed, if it should forget that the good of the whole can
only be promoted by advancing the good of each of the
parts or members which compose the whole. It will not
be in the power of the president and senate to make
any treaties, by which they and their families and es-
tates will not be equally bound and affected with the
rest of the community; and having no private interest
distinct from that of the nation, they will be under no
temptations to neglect the latter.

As to corruption, the case is not supposable, he must
either have been very unfortunate in his intercourse
with the world, or possess a heart very susceptible of
such impressions, who can think it probable that the
president and two-thirds of the senate will ever be capable of such unworthy conduct. The idea is too gross
and too invidious to be entertained. But in such a case,
if it should ever happen, the treaty so obtained from us

would, like all other fraudulent contracts, be null and void by the laws of nations.

With respect to their responsibility, it is difficult to conceive how it could be encreased. Every consideration that can influence the human mind, such as honor, oaths, reputation, conscience, the love of country, and family affections and attachments, afford security for their fidelity. In short, as the constitution has taken the utmost care that they shall be men of talents and integrity, we have reason to be persuaded that the treaties they make will be as advantageous as all circumstances considered could be made; and so far as the fear of punishment and disgrace can operate, that motive to good behaviour is amply afforded by the article on the subject of impeachments.

PUBLIUS.

THE FEDERALIST NO. 70

ALEXANDER HAMILTON

MARCH 15, 1788

To the People of the State of New York.

There is an idea, which is not without its advocates, that a vigorous executive is inconsistent with the genius of republican government. The enlightened well wishers to this species of government must at least hope that the supposition is destitute of foundation; since they can never admit its truth, without at the same time admitting the condemnation of their own principles.

Energy in the executive is a leading character in the definition of good government. It is essential to the protection of the community against foreign attacks: It is not less essential to the steady administration of the laws, to the protection of property against those irregular and high handed combinations, which sometimes interrupt the ordinary course of justice, to the security of liberty against the enterprises and assaults of ambition, of faction and of anarchy. Every man the least conversant in Roman story knows how often that republic was obliged to take refuge in the absolute power of a single man, under the formidable title of dictator, as well against the intrigues of ambitious individuals, who aspired to the tyranny, and the seditions of whole classes of the community, whose conduct threatened the existence of all government, as against the invasions of external enemies, who menaced the conquest and destruction of Rome.

There can be no need however to multiply arguments or examples on this head. A feeble executive implies a feeble execution of the government. A feeble execution is but another phrase for a bad execution: And a government ill executed, whatever it may be in theory, must be in practice a bad government.

Taking it for granted, therefore, that all men of sense will agree in the necessity of an energetic executive; it will only remain to inquire, what are the ingredients which constitute this energy—how far can they be combined with those other ingredients which constitute safety in the republican sense? And how far does this combination characterise the plan, which has been reported by the convention?

The ingredients, which constitute energy in the executive, are first unity, secondly duration, thirdly an adequate provision for its support, fourthly competent powers.

The circumstances which constitute safety in the republican sense are, Ist. a due dependence on the people, secondly a due responsibility.

Those politicians and statesmen, who have been the most celebrated for the soundness of their principles, and for the justness of their views, have declared in favor of a single executive and a numerous legislature. They have with great propriety considered energy as the most necessary qualification of the former, and have regarded this as most applicable to power in a single hand; while they have with equal propriety considered the latter as best adapted to deliberation and wisdom, and best calculated to conciliate the confidence of the people and to secure their privileges and interests.

That unity is conducive to energy will not be disputed. Decision, activity, secrecy, and dispatch will generally characterise the proceedings of one man, in a much more eminent degree, than the proceedings of any greater number; and in proportion as the number is increased, these qualities will be diminished.

This unity may be destroyed in two ways; either by vesting the power in two or more magistrates of equal dignity and authority; or by vesting it ostensibly in one man, subject in whole or in part to the controul and co-operation of others, in the capacity of counsellors to him. Of the first the two consuls of Rome may serve as an example; of the last we shall find examples in the constitutions of several of the states. New-York and New-Jersey, if I recollect right, are the only states, which have entrusted the executive authority wholly to single men.* Both these methods of destroying the unity of the executive have their partisans; but the votaries of an executive council are the most numerous. They are both liable, if not to equal, to similar objections; and may in most lights be examined in conjunction.

The experience of other nations will afford little instruction on this head. As far however as it teaches any thing, it teaches us not to be inamoured of plurality in the executive. We have seen that the Achaeans on an experiment of two Praetors, were induced to abolish one. The Roman history records many instances of mischiefs to the republic from the dissentions between the consuls, and between the military tribunes, who were at times substituted to the consuls. But it gives us no specimens of any peculiar advantages derived to the state, from the circumstance of the plurality of those magistrates. That the dissentions between them were not more frequent, or more fatal, is matter of astonishment; until we advert to the singular position in which the republic was almost continually placed and to the prudent policy pointed out by the circumstances of the state, and pursued by the consuls, of making a division of the government between them. The Patricians engaged in a perpetual struggle with the Plebians for the preservation of their antient authorities and dignities; the consuls, who were generally chosen out

---

* *New-York has no council except for the single purpose of appointing to offices; New-Jersey has a council, whom the governor may consult. But I think from the terms of the constitution their resolutions do not bind him.* (Publius)

of the former body, were commonly united by the personal interest they had in the defence of the privileges of their order. In addition to this motive of union, after the arms of the republic had considerably expanded the bounds of its empire, it became an established custom with the consuls to divide the administration between themselves by lot; one of them remaining at Rome to govern the city and its environs; the other taking the command in the more distant provinces. This expedient must no doubt have had great influence in preventing those collisions and rivalships, which might otherwise have embroiled the peace of the republic.

But quitting the dim light of historical research, and attaching ourselves purely to the dictates of reason and good sense, we shall discover much greater cause to reject than to approve the idea of plurality in the executive, under any modification whatever.

Wherever two or more persons are engaged in any common enterprize or pursuit, there is always danger of difference of opinion. If it be a public trust or office in which they are cloathed with equal dignity and authority, there is peculiar danger of personal emulation and even animosity. From either and especially from all these causes, the most bitter dissentions are apt to spring. Whenever these happen, they lessen the respectability, weaken the authority, and distract the plans and operations of those whom they divide. If they should unfortunately assail the supreme executive magistracy of a country, consisting of a plurality of persons, they might impede or frustrate the most important measures of the government, in the most critical emergencies of the state. And what is still worse, they might split the community into the most violent and irreconcilable factions, adhering differently to the different individuals who composed the magistracy.

Men often oppose a thing merely because they have had no agency in planning it, or because it may have been planned by those whom they dislike. But if they have been consulted and have happened to disapprove, opposition then becomes in their estimation an indispensable duty of self love. They seem to think themselves bound in honor, and by all the motives of personal infallibility to defeat the success of what has been resolved upon, contrary to their sentiments. Men of upright, benevolent tempers have too many opportunities of remarking with horror, to what desperate lengths this disposition is sometimes carried, and how often the great interests of society are sacrificed to the vanity, to the conceit and to the obstinacy of individuals, who have credit enough to make their passions and their caprices interesting to mankind. Perhaps the question now before the public may in its consequences afford melancholy proofs of the effects of this despicable frailty, or rather detestable vice in the human character.

Upon the principles of a free government, inconveniencies from the source just mentioned must necessarily be submitted to in the formation of the legislature; but it is unnecessary and therefore unwise to introduce them into the constitution of the executive. It is here too that they may be most pernicious. In the legislature, promptitude of decision is oftener an evil than a benefit. The differences of opinion, and the jarrings of parties in that department of the government, though they may sometimes obstruct salutary plans, yet often promote deliberation and circumspection; and serve to check excesses in the majority. When a resolution too is once taken, the opposition must be at an end. That resolution is a law, and resistance to it punishable. But no favourable circumstances palliate or atone for the disadvantages of dissention in the executive department. Here they are pure and unmixed. There is no point at which they cease to operate. They serve to embarrass and weaken the execution of the plan or measure, to which they relate, from the first step to the final conclusion of it. They constantly counteract those qualities in the executive, which are the most necessary ingredients in its composition, vigour and expedition, and this without any counterbalancing good. In the conduct of war, in which the energy of the executive is the bulwark of the national security, every thing would be to be apprehended from its plurality.

It must be confessed that these observations apply with principal weight to the first case supposed, that is to a plurality of magistrates of equal dignity and authority; a scheme the advocates for which are not likely to form a numerous sect: But they apply, though not with equal, yet with considerable weight, to the project of a council, whose concurrence is made constitutionally necessary to the operations of the ostensible executive. An artful cabal in that council would be able to distract and to enervate the whole system of administration. If no such cabal should exist, the mere diversity of views and opinions would alone be sufficient to tincture the exercise of the executive authority with a spirit of habitual feebleness and dilatoriness.

But one of the weightiest objections to a plurality in the executive, and which lies as much against the last as the first plan, is that it tends to conceal faults, and destroy responsibility. Responsibility is of two kinds, to censure and to punishment. The first is the most important of the two; especially in an elective office. Man, in public trust, will much oftener act in such a manner as to render him unworthy of being any longer trusted, than in such a manner as to make him obnoxious to legal punishment. But the multiplication of the executive adds to the difficulty of detection in either case. It often becomes impossible, amidst mutual accusations, to determine on whom the blame or the punishment of a pernicious measure, or series of pernicious measures ought really to fall. It is shifted from one to another with so much dexterity, and under such plausible appearances, that the public opinion is left in suspense about the real author. The circumstances which may have led to any national miscarriage or misfortune are sometimes so complicated, that where there are a number of actors who may have had different degrees and kinds of agency, though we may clearly see upon the whole that there has been mismanagement, yet it may be impracticable to pronounce to whose account the evil which may have been incurred is truly chargeable.

"I was overruled by my council. The council were so divided in their opinions, that it was impossible to obtain any better resolution on the point." These and similar pretexts are constantly at hand, whether true or false. And who is there that will either take the trouble or incur the odium of a strict scrutiny into the secret springs of the transaction? Should there be found a citizen zealous enough to undertake the unpromising task, if there happen to be a collusion between the parties concerned, how easy is it to cloath the circumstances with so much ambiguity, as to render it uncertain what was the precise conduct of any of those parties?

In the single instance in which the governor of this state is coupled with a council, that is in the appointment to offices, we have seen the mischiefs of it in the view now under consideration. Scandalous appointments to important offices have been made. Some cases indeed have been so flagrant, that ALL PARTIES have agreed in the impropriety of the thing. When enquiry has been made, the blame has been laid by the governor on the members of the council; who on their part have charged it upon his nomination: While the people remain altogether at a loss to determine by whose influence their interests have been committed to hands so unqualified, and so manifestly improper. In tenderness to individuals, I forbear to descend to particulars.

It is evident from these considerations, that the plurality of the executive tends to deprive the people of the two greatest securities they can have for the faithful exercise of any delegated power; first, the restraints of public opinion, which lose their efficacy as well on account of the division of the censure attendant on bad measures among a number, as on account of the uncertainty on whom it ought to fall; and secondly, the opportunity of discovering with facility and clearness the misconduct of the persons they trust, in order either to their removal from office, or to their actual punishment, in cases which admit of it.

In England the king is a perpetual magistrate; and it is a maxim, which has obtained for the sake of the public peace, that he is unaccountable for his administration, and his person sacred. Nothing therefore can be wiser in that kingdom than to annex to the king a constitutional council, who may be responsible to the nation for the advice they give. Without this there would be no responsibility whatever in the executive department; an idea inadmissible in a free government. But even there the king is not bound by the resolutions of his council, though they are answerable for the advice they give. He is the absolute master of his own conduct, in the exercise of his office; and may observe or disregard the council given to him at his sole discretion.

But in a republic, where every magistrate ought to be personally responsible for his behaviour in office, the reason which in the British constitution dictates the propriety of a council not only ceases to apply, but turns against the institution. In the monarchy of Great-Britain, it furnishes a substitute for the prohibited responsibility of the chief magistrate; which serves in some degree as a hostage to the national justice for his good behaviour. In the American republic it would serve to destroy, or would greatly diminish the intended and necessary responsibility of the chief magistrate himself.

The idea of a council to the executive, which has so generally obtained in the state constitutions, has been derived from that maxim of republican jealousy, which considers power as safer in the hands of a number of men than of a single man. If the maxim should be admitted to be applicable to the case, I should contend that the advantage on that side would not counterbalance the numerous disadvantages on the opposite side.

But I do not think the rule at all applicable to the executive power. I clearly concur in opinion in this particular with a writer whom the celebrated Junius pronounces to be "deep, solid and ingenious," that, "the executive power is more easily confined when it is one":* That it is far more safe there should be a single object for the jealousy and watchfulness of the people; and in a word that all multiplication of the executive is rather dangerous than friendly to liberty.

A little consideration will satisfy us, that the species of security sought for in the multiplication of the executive is unattainable. Numbers must be so great as to render combination difficult; or they are rather a source of danger than of security. The united credit and influence of several individuals must be more formidable to liberty than the credit and influence of either of them separately. When power therefore is placed in the hands of so small a number of men, as to admit of their interests and views being easily combined in a common enterprise, by an artful leader, it becomes more liable to abuse and more dangerous when abused, than if it be lodged in the hands of one man; who from the very circumstance of his being alone will be more narrowly watched and more readily suspected, and who cannot unite so great a mass of influence as when he is associated with others. The Decemvirs of Rome, whose name denotes their number,† were more to be dreaded in their usurpation than any ONE of them would have been. No person would think of proposing an executive much more numerous than that body, from six to a dozen have been suggested for the number of the council. The extreme of these numbers is not too great for an easy combination; and from such a combination America would have more to fear, than from the ambition of any single individual. A council to a magistrate, who is himself responsible for what he does, are generally nothing better than a clog upon his good intentions; are often the instruments and accomplices of his bad, and are almost always a cloak to his faults.

I forbear to dwell upon the subject of expence; though it be evident that if the council should be numerous enough to answer the principal end, aimed at by the institution, the salaries of the members, who must be drawn from their homes to reside at the seat of government, would form an item in the catalogue of public expenditures, too serious to be incurred for an object of equivocal utility.

I will only add, that prior to the appearance of the constitution, I rarely met with an intelligent man from any of the states, who did hot admit as the result of experience, that the UNITY of the Executive of this state was one of the best of the distinguishing features of our constitution.

PUBLIUS.

THE FEDERALIST NO. 78

ALEXANDER HAMILTON

MAY 28, 1788

We proceed now to an examination of the judiciary department of the proposed government.

In unfolding the defects of the existing confederation, the utility and necessity of a federal judicature have been clearly pointed out. It is the less necessary to recapitulate the considerations there urged; as the propriety of the institution in the abstract is not disputed: The only questions which have been raised being relative to the manner of constituting it, and to its extent. To these points therefore our observations shall be confined.

The manner of constituting it seems to embrace these several objects—1st. The mode of appointing the judges. 2d. The tenure by which they are to hold their places. 3d. The partition of the judiciary authority between different courts, and their relations to each other.

First. As to the mode of appointing the judges: This is the same with that of appointing the officers of the union in general, and has been so fully discussed in the two last numbers, that nothing can be said here which would not be useless repetition.

Second. As to the tenure by which the judges are to hold their places: This chiefly concerns their duration in office; the provisions for their support; and the precautions for their responsibility.

According to the plan of the convention, all the judges who may be appointed by the United States are to hold their offices *during good behaviour,* which is conformable to the most approved of the state constitutions; and among the rest, to that of this state. Its propriety having been drawn into question by the adversaries of that plan, is no light symptom of the rage for objection which disorders their imaginations and judgments. The standard of good behaviour for the continuance in office of the judicial magistracy is certainly one of the most valuable of the modern improvements in the practice of government. In a monarchy it is an excellent barrier to the despotism of the prince: In a republic it is a no less excellent barrier to the encroachments and oppressions of the representative body. And it is the best expedient which can be devised in any government, to secure a steady, upright and impartial administration of the laws.

Whoever attentively considers the different departments of power must perceive, that in a government in which they are separated from each other, the judiciary, from the nature of its functions, will always be the least dangerous to the political rights of the constitution; because it will be least in a capacity to annoy or injure them. The executive not only dispenses the honors, but holds the sword of the community. The legislature not only commands the purse, but prescribes the rules by which the duties and rights of every citizen are to be regulated. The judiciary on the contrary has no influence over either the sword or the purse, no direction either of the strength or of the wealth of the society, and can take no active resolution whatever. It may truly be said to have neither Force nor Will, but merely judgment; and must ultimately depend upon the aid of the executive arm even for the efficacy of its judgments.

This simple view of the matter suggests several important consequences. It proves incontestibly that the judiciary is beyond comparison the weakest of the three departments of power;* that it can never attack with success either of the other two; and that all possible care is requisite to enable it to defend itself against their attacks. It equally proves, that though individual oppression may now and then proceed from the courts of justice, the general liberty of the people can never be endangered from that quarter: I mean, so long as the judiciary remains truly distinct from both the legislative and executive. For I agree that "there is no liberty, if the power of judging be not separated from the legislative and executive powers."† And it proves, in the last place, that as liberty can have nothing to fear from the judiciary alone, but would have every thing to fear from its union with either of the other departments; that as all the effects of such an union must ensue from a dependence of the former on the latter, notwithstanding a nominal and apparent separation; that as from the natural feebleness of the judiciary, it is in continual jeopardy of being overpowered, awed or influenced by its coordinate branches; and that as nothing can contribute so much to its firmness and independence, as permanency in office, this quality may therefore be justly regarded as an indispensable ingredient

---

* *The celebrated Montesquieu speaking of them says, "of the three powers above mentioned, the JUDICIARY is next to nothing." Spirit of Laws, vol. 1, page 186. (Publius)*
† *Idem. page 181. (Publius)*

in its constitution; and in a great measure as the citadel of the public justice and the public security.

The complete independence of the courts of justice is peculiarly essential in a limited constitution. By a limited constitution I understand one which contains certain specified exceptions to the legislative authority; such for instance as that it shall pass no bills of attainder, no *ex post facto* laws, and the like. Limitations of this kind can be preserved in practice no other way than through the medium of the courts of justice; whose duty it must be to declare all acts contrary to the manifest tenor of the constitution void. Without this, all the reservations of particular rights or privileges would amount to nothing.

Some perplexity respecting the right of the courts to pronounce legislative acts void, because contrary to the constitution, has arisen from an imagination that the doctrine would imply a superiority of the judiciary to the legislative power. It is urged that the authority which can declare the acts of another void, must necessarily be superior to the one whose acts may be declared void. As this doctrine is of great importance in all the American constitutions, a brief discussion of the grounds on which it rests cannot be unacceptable.

There is no position which depends on clearer principles, than that every act of a delegated authority, contrary to the tenor of the commission under which it is exercised, is void. No legislative act therefore contrary to the constitution can be valid. To deny this would be to affirm that the deputy is greater than his principal; that the servant is above his master; that the representatives of the people are superior to the people themselves; that men acting by virtue of powers may do not only what their powers do not authorise, but what they forbid.

If it be said that the legislative body are themselves the constitutional judges of their own powers, and that the construction they put upon them is conclusive upon the other departments, it may be answered, that this cannot be the natural presumption, where it is not to be collected from any particular provisions in the constitution. It is not otherwise to be supposed that the constitution could intend to enable the representatives of the people to substitute their *will* to that of their constituents. It is far more rational to suppose that the courts were designed to be an intermediate body between the people and the legislature, in order, among other things, to keep the latter within the limits assigned to their authority. The interpretation of the laws is the proper and peculiar province of the courts. A constitution is in fact, and must be, regarded by the judges as a fundamental law. It therefore belongs to them to ascertain its meaning as well as the meaning of any particular act proceeding from the legislative body. If there should happen to be an irreconcileable variance between the two, that which has the superior obligation and validity ought of course to be preferred; or in other words, the constitution ought to be preferred to the statute, the intention of the people to the intention of their agents.

Nor does this conclusion by any means suppose a superiority of the judicial to the legislative power. It only supposes that the power of the people is superior to both; and that where the will of the legislature declared in its statutes, stands in opposition to that of the people declared in the constitution, the judges ought to be governed by the latter, rather than the former. They ought to regulate their decisions by the fundamental laws, rather than by those which are not fundamental.

This exercise of judicial discretion in determining between two contradictory laws, is exemplified in a familiar instance. It not uncommonly happens, that there are two statutes existing at one time, clashing in whole or in part with each other, and neither of them containing any repealing clause or expression. In such a case, it is the province of the courts to liquidate and fix their meaning and operation: So far as they can by any fair construction be reconciled to each other; reason and law conspire to dictate that this should be done. Where this is impracticable, it becomes a matter of necessity to give effect to one, in exclusion of the other. The rule which has obtained in the courts for determining their relative validity is that the last in order of time shall be preferred to the first. But this is mere rule of construction, not derived from any positive law, but from the nature and reason of the thing. It is a rule not enjoined upon the courts by legislative provision, but adopted by themselves, as consonant to truth and propriety, for the direction of their conduct as interpreters of the law. They thought it reasonable, that between the interfering acts of an *equal* authority, that which was the last indication of its will, should have the preference.

But in regard to the interfering acts of a superior and subordinate authority, of an original and derivative power, the nature and reason of the thing indicate the converse of that rule as proper to be followed. They teach us that the prior act of a superior ought to be preferred to the subsequent act of an inferior and subordinate authority; and that, accordingly, whenever a particular statute contravenes the constitution, it will be the duty of the judicial tribunals to adhere to the latter, and disregard the former.

It can be of no weight to say, that the courts on the pretence of a repugnancy, may substitute their own pleasure to the constitutional intentions of the legislature. This might as well happen in the case of two contradictory statutes; or it might as well happen in every adjudication upon any single statute. The courts must declare the sense of the law; and if they should be disposed to exercise WILL instead of JUDGMENT, the consequence would equally be the substitution of their pleasure to that of the legislative body. The observation, if it proved any thing, would prove that there ought to be no judges distinct from that body.

If then the courts of justice are to be considered as the bulwarks of a limited constitution against legislative encroachments, this consideration will afford a strong argument for the permanent tenure of judicial offices, since nothing will contribute so much as this to that independent spirit in the judges, which must be essential to the faithful performance of so arduous a duty.

This independence of the judges is equally requisite to guard the constitution and the rights of individuals from the effects of those ill humours which the arts of designing men, or the influence of particular conjunctures, sometimes disseminate among the people themselves, and which, though they speedily give place to better information and more deliberate reflection, have a tendency in the mean time to occasion dangerous innovations in the government, and serious oppressions of the minor party in the community. Though I trust the friends of the proposed constitution will never concur with its enemies* in questioning that fundamental principle of republican government, which admits the right of the people to alter or abolish the established constitution whenever they find it inconsistent with their happiness; yet it is not to be inferred from this principle, that the representatives of the people, whenever a momentary inclination happens to lay hold of a majority of their constituents incompatible with the provisions in the existing constitution, would on that account be justifiable in a violation of those provisions; or that the courts would be under a greater obligation to connive at infractions in this shape, than when they had proceeded wholly from the cabals of the representative body. Until the people have by some solemn and authoritative act annulled or changed the established form, it is binding upon themselves collectively, as well as individually; and no presumption, or even knowledge of their sentiments, can warrant their representatives in a departure from it, prior to such an act. But it is easy to see that it would require an uncommon portion of fortitude in the judges to do their duty as faithful guardians of the constitution, where legislative invasions of it had been instigated by the major voice of the community.

But it is not with a view to infractions of the constitution only that the independence of the judges may be an essential safeguard against the effects of occasional

---

* *Vide Protest of the minority of the convention of Pennsylvania, Martin's speech, &c. (Publius)*

ill humours in the society. These sometimes extend no farther than to the injury of the private rights of particular classes of citizens, by unjust and partial laws. Here also the firmness of the judicial magistracy is of vast importance in mitigating the severity, and confining the operation of such laws. It not only serves to moderate the immediate mischiefs of those which may have been passed, but it operates as a check upon the legislative body in passing them; who, perceiving that obstacles to the success of an iniquitous intention are to be expected from the scruples of the courts, are in a manner compelled by the very motives of the injustice they meditate, to qualify their attempts. This is a circumstance calculated to have more influence upon the character of our governments, than but few may be aware of. The benefits of the integrity and moderation of the judiciary have already been felt in more states than one; and though they may have displeased those whose sinister expectations they may have disappointed, they must have commanded the esteem and applause of all the virtuous and disinterested. Considerate men of every description ought to prize whatever will tend to beget or fortify that temper in the courts; as no man can be sure that he may not be tomorrow the victim of a spirit of injustice, by which he may be a gainer to-day. And every man must now feel that the inevitable tendency of such a spirit is to sap the foundations of public and private confidence, and to introduce in its stead, universal distrust and distress.

That inflexible and uniform adherence to the rights of the constitution and of individuals, which we perceive to be indispensable in the courts of justice, can certainly not be expected from judges who hold their offices by a temporary commission. Periodical appointments, however regulated, or by whomsoever made, would in some way or other be fatal to their necessary independence. If the power of making them was committed either to the executive or legislature, there would be danger of an improper complaisance to the branch which possessed it; if to both, there would be an unwillingness to hazard the displeasure of either; if to the people, or to persons chosen by them for the special purpose, there would be too great a disposition to consult popularity, to justify a reliance that nothing would be consulted but the constitution and the laws.

There is yet a further and a weighty reason for the permanency of the judicial offices; which is deducible from the nature of the qualifications they require. It has been frequently remarked with great propriety, that a voluminous code of laws is one of the inconveniences necessarily connected with the advantages of a free government. To avoid an arbitrary discretion in the courts, it is indispensable that they should be bound down by strict rules and precedents, which serve to define and point out their duty in every particular case that comes before them; and it will readily be conceived from the variety of controversies which grow out of the folly and wickedness of mankind, that the records of those precedents must unavoidably swell to a very considerable bulk, and must demand long and laborious study to acquire a competent knowledge of them. Hence it is that there can be but few men in the society, who will have sufficient skill in the laws to qualify them for the stations of judges. And making the proper deductions for the ordinary depravity of human nature, the number must be still smaller of those who unite the requisite integrity with the requisite knowledge. These considerations apprise us, that the government can have no great option between fit characters; and that a temporary duration in office, which would naturally discourage such characters from quitting a lucrative line of practice to accept a seat on the bench, would have a tendency to throw the administration of justice into hands less able, and less well qualified to conduct it with utility and dignity. In the present circumstances of this country, and in those in which it is likely to be for a long time to come, the disadvantages on this score would be greater than they may at first sight appear; but it must be confessed that they are far inferior to those which present themselves under the other aspects of the subject.

Upon the whole there can be no room to doubt that the convention acted wisely in copying from the models of those constitutions which have established *good behaviour* as the tenure of their judicial offices in point of duration; and that so far from being blameable on this account, their plan would have been inexcuseably defective if it had wanted this important feature of good government. The experience of Great Britain affords an illustrious comment on the excellence of the institution.

PUBLIUS.

ALEXANDER HAMILTON

MAY 28, 1788

In the course of the foregoing review of the constitution I have taken notice of, and endeavoured to answer, most of the objections which have appeared against it. There however remain a few which either did not fall naturally under any particular head, or were forgotten in their proper places. These shall now be discussed; but as the subject has been drawn into great length, I shall so far consult brevity as to comprise all my observations on these miscellaneous points in a single paper.

The most considerable of these remaining objections is, that the plan of the convention contains no bill of rights. Among other answers given to this, it has been upon different occasions remarked, that the constitutions of several of the states are in a similar predicament. I add, that New-York is of this number. And yet the opposers of the new system in this state, who profess an unlimited admiration for its constitution, are among the most intemperate partizans of a bill of rights. To justify their zeal in this matter, they alledge two things; one is, that though the constitution of New-York has no bill of rights prefixed to it, yet it contains in the body of it various provisions in favour of particular privileges and rights, which in substance amount to the same thing; the other is, that the constitution adopts in their full extent the common and statute law of Great-Britain, by which many other rights not expressed in it are equally secured.

To the first I answer, that the constitution proposed by the convention contains, as well as the constitution of this state, a number of such provisions.

Independent of those, which relate to the structure of the government, we find the following: Article I. section 3. clause 7. "Judgment in cases of impeachment shall not extend further than to removal from office, and disqualification to hold and enjoy any office of honour, trust or profit under the United States; but the party convicted shall nevertheless be liable and subject to indictment, trial, judgment and punishment, according to law." Section 9. of the same article, clause 2. "The privilege of the writ of *habeas corpus* shall not be suspended, unless when in cases of rebellion or invasion the public safety may require it." Clause 3. "No bill of attainder or *ex post facto* law shall be passed." Clause 7. "No title of nobility shall be granted by the United States: And no person holding any office of profit or trust under them, shall, without the consent of the congress, accept of any present, emolument, office or title, of any kind whatever, from any king, prince or foreign state." Article III. section 2. clause 3. "The trial of all crimes, except in cases of impeachment, shall be by jury; and such trial shall be held in the state where the said crimes shall have been committed; but when not committed within any state, the trial shall be at such place or places as the congress may by law have directed." Section 3, of the same article, "Treason against the United States shall consist only in levying war against them, or in adhering to their enemies, giving them aid and comfort. No person shall be convicted of treason unless on the testimony of two witnesses to the same overt act, or on confession in open court." And clause 3, of the same section. "The congress shall have power to declare the punishment of treason, but no attainder of treason shall work corruption of blood, or forfeiture, except during the life of the person attainted."

It may well be a question whether these are not upon the whole, of equal importance with any which are to be found in the constitution of this state. The establishment of the writ of *habeas corpus*, the prohibition of *ex post facto* laws, and of TITLES OF NOBILITY, *to which we have no corresponding provisions in our constitution*, are perhaps greater securities to liberty and republicanism than any it contains. The creation of crimes after the commission of the fact, or in other words, the subjecting of men to punishment for things which, when they were done, were breaches of no law, and the practice of arbitrary imprisonments have been in all ages the favourite and most formidable instruments of tyranny. The observations of the judicious Blackstone* in reference to the latter, are well worthy of recital. "To bereave a man of life (says he) or by violence to confiscate his estate, without accusation or trial, would be so gross and notorious an act of despotism, as must at once convey the alarm of tyranny throughout the whole nation; but confinement of the person by secretly hurrying him to goal, where his sufferings are unknown or forgotten, is a less public, a less striking, and therefore a *more dangerous engine* of arbitrary government." And as a remedy for this fatal evil, he is every where peculiarly

---

* *Vide Blackstone's Commentaries, vol. 1, page 136. (Publius)*

emphatical in his encomiums on the *habeas corpus* act, which in one place he calls "the BULWARK of the British constitution."*

Nothing need be said to illustrate the importance of the prohibition of titles of nobility. This may truly be denominated the corner stone of republican government; for so long as they are excluded, there can never be serious danger that the government will be any other than that of the people.

To the second, that is, to the pretended establishment of the common and statute law by the constitution, I answer, that they are expressly made subject "to such alterations and provisions as the legislature shall from time to time make concerning the same." They are therefore at any moment liable to repeal by the ordinary legislative power, and of course have no constitutional sanction. The only use of the declaration was to recognize the ancient law, and to remove doubts which might have been occasioned by the revolution. This consequently can be considered as no part of a declaration of rights, which under our constitutions must be intended as limitations of the power of the government itself.

It has been several times truly remarked, that bills of rights are in their origin, stipulations between kings and their subjects, abridgments of prerogative in favor of privilege, reservations of rights not surrendered to the prince. Such was MAGNA CHARTA, obtained by the Barons, sword in hand, from king John. Such were the subsequent confirmations of that charter by subsequent princes. Such was the *petition of right* assented to by

---

* *Idem, vol. 4, page 438. (Publius)*

Charles the First, in the beginning of his reign. Such also was the declaration of right presented by the lords and commons to the prince of Orange in 1688, and afterwards thrown into the form of an act of parliament, called the bill of rights. It is evident, therefore, that according to their primitive signification, they have no application to constitutions professedly founded upon the power of the people, and executed by their immediate representatives and servants. Here, in strictness, the people surrender nothing, and as they retain every thing, they have no need of particular reservations. "WE THE PEOPLE of the United States, to secure the blessings of liberty to ourselves and our posterity, do *ordain* and *establish* this constitution for the United States of America." Here is a better recognition of popular rights than volumes of those aphorisms which make the principal figure in several of our state bills of rights, and which would sound much better in a treatise of ethics than in a constitution of government.

But a minute detail of particular rights is certainly far less applicable to a constitution like that under consideration, which is merely intended to regulate the general political interests of the nation, than to a constitution which has the regulation of every species of personal and private concerns. If therefore the loud clamours against the plan of the convention on this score, are well founded, no epithets of reprobation will be too strong for the constitution of this state. But the truth is, that both of them contain all, which in relation to their objects, is reasonably to be desired.

I go further, and affirm that bills of rights, in the sense and in the extent in which they are contended for, are not only unnecessary in the proposed constitution, but would even be dangerous. They would contain various exceptions to powers which are not granted; and on this very account, would afford a colourable pretext to claim more than were granted. For why declare that things shall not be done which there is no power to do? Why for instance, should it be said, that the liberty of the press shall not be restrained, when no power is given by which restrictions may be imposed? I will not contend that such a provision would confer a regulating power; but it is evident that it would furnish, to men disposed to usurp, a plausible pretence for claiming that power. They might urge with a semblance of reason, that the constitution ought not to be charged with the absurdity of providing against the abuse of an authority, which was not given, and that the provision against restraining the liberty of the press afforded a clear implication, that a power to prescribe proper regulations concerning it, was intended to be vested in the national government. This may serve as a specimen of the numerous handles which would be given to the doctrine of constructive powers, by the indulgence of an injudicious zeal for bills of rights.

On the subject of the liberty of the press, as much has been said, I cannot forbear adding a remark or two: In the first place, I observe that there is not a syllable concerning it in the constitution of this state, and in the next, I contend that whatever has been said about it in that of any other state, amounts to nothing. What signifies a declaration that "the liberty of the press shall be inviolably preserved?" What is the liberty of the press? Who can give it any definition which would not leave the utmost latitude for evasion? I hold it to be impracticable; and from this, I infer, that its security, whatever fine declarations may be inserted in any constitution respecting it, must altogether depend on public opinion, and on the general spirit of the people and of the government.* And here, after all, as intimated upon another occasion, must we seek for the only solid basis of all our rights.

There remains but one other view of this matter to conclude the point. The truth is, after all the declamation we have heard, that the constitution is itself in every rational sense, and to every useful purpose, A BILL OF RIGHTS. The several bills of rights, in Great-Britain, form its constitution, and conversely the constitution of each state is its bill of rights. And the proposed constitution, if adopted, will be the bill of rights of the union. Is it one object of a bill of rights to declare and specify the political privileges of the citi-

---

* *To show that there is a power in the constitution by which the liberty of the press may be affected, recourse has been had to the power of taxation. It is said that duties may be laid upon publications so high as to amount to a prohibition. I know not by what logic it could be maintained that the declarations in the state constitutions, in favour of the freedom of the press, would be a constitutional impediment to the imposition of duties upon publications by the state legislatures. It cannot certainly be pretended that any degree of duties, however low, would be an abrigement of the liberty of the press. We know that newspapers are taxed in Great-Britain, and yet it is notorious that the press no where enjoys greater liberty than in that country. And if duties of any kind may be laid without a violation of that liberty, it is evident that the extent must depend on legislative discretion, regulated by public opinion; so that after all, general declarations respecting the liberty of the press will give it no greater security than it will have without them. The same invasions of it may be effected under the state constitutions which contain those declarations through the means of taxation, as under the proposed constitution which has nothing of the kind. It would be quite as significant to declare that government ought to be free, that taxes ought not to be excessive, &c., as that the liberty of the press ought not to be restrained. (Publius)*

zens in the structure and administration of the government? This is done in the most ample and precise manner in the plan of the convention, comprehending various precautions for the public security, which are not to be found in any of the state constitutions. Is another object of a bill of rights to define certain immunities and modes of proceeding, which are relative to personal and private concerns? This we have seen has also been attended to, in a variety of cases, in the same plan. Adverting therefore to the substantial meaning of a bill of rights, it is absurd to allege that it is not to be found in the work of the convention. It may be said that it does not go far enough, though it will not be easy to make this appear; but it can with no propriety be contended that there is no such thing. It certainly must be immaterial what mode is observed as to the order of declaring the rights of the citizens, if they are to be found in any part of the instrument which establishes the government. And hence it must be apparent that much of what has been said on this subject rests merely on verbal and nominal distinctions, which are entirely foreign from the substance of the thing.

Another objection, which has been made, and which from the frequency of its repetition it is to be presumed is relied on, is of this nature:—It is improper (say the objectors) to confer such large powers, as are proposed, upon the national government; because the seat of that government must of necessity be too remote from many of the states to admit of a proper knowledge on the part of the constituent, of the conduct of the representative body. This argument, if it proves any thing, proves that there ought to be no general government whatever. For the powers which it seems to be agreed on all hands, ought to be vested in the union, cannot be safely intrusted to a body which is not under every requisite controul. But there are satisfactory reasons to shew that the objection is in reality not well founded. There is in most of the arguments which relate to distance a palpable illusion of the imagination. What are the sources of information by which the people in Montgomery county must regulate their judgment of the conduct of their representatives in the state legislature? Of personal observation they can have no benefit. This is confined to the citizens on the spot. They must therefore depend on the information of intelligent men, in whom they confide—and how must these men obtain their information? Evidently from the complection of public measures, from the public prints, from correspondences with their representatives, and with other persons who reside at the place of their deliberation. This does not apply to Montgomery county only, but to all the counties, at any considerable distance from the seat of government.

It is equally evident that the same sources of information would be open to the people, in relation to the conduct of their representatives in the general government; and the impediments to a prompt communication which distance may be supposed to create, will be overbalanced by the effects of the vigilance of the state governments. The executive and legislative bodies of each state will be so many centinels over the persons employed in every department of the national administration; and as it will be in their power to adopt and pursue a regular and effectual system of intelligence, they can never be at a loss to know the behaviour of those who represent their constituents in the national councils, and can readily communicate the same knowledge to the people. Their disposition to apprise the community of whatever may prejudice its interests from another quarter, may be relied upon, if it were only from the rivalship of power. And we may conclude with the fullest assurance, that the people, through that channel, will be better informed of the conduct of their national representatives, than they can be by any means they now possess of that of their state representatives.

It ought also to be remembered, that the citizens who inhabit the country at and near the seat of government, will in all questions that affect the general liberty and prosperity, have the same interest with those who are at a distance; and that they will stand ready to sound the alarm when necessary, and to point out the actors in any pernicious project. The public papers will be expeditious messengers of intelligence to the most remote inhabitants of the union.

Among the many extraordinary objections which have appeared against the proposed constitution, the most extraordinary and the least colourable one, is derived from the want of some provision respecting the debts due *to* the United States. This has been represented as a tacit relinquishment of those debts, and as a wicked contrivance to screen public defaulters. The newspapers have teemed with the most inflammatory railings on this head; and yet there is nothing clearer than that the suggestion is entirely void of foundation, and is the offspring of extreme ignorance or extreme dishonesty. In addition to the remarks I have made upon the subject in another place, I shall only observe, that as it is a plain dictate of common sense, so it is also an established doctrine of political law, that "*States neither lose any of their rights, nor are discharged from any of their obligations by a change in the form of their civil government.*"*

The last objection of any consequence which I at present recollect, turns upon the article of expence. If it were even true that the adoption of the proposed government would occasion a considerable increase of expence, it would be an objection that ought to have no weight against the plan. The great bulk of the citizens of America, are with reason convinced that union is the basis of their political happiness. Men of sense of all parties now, with few exceptions, agree that it cannot be preserved under the present system, nor without radical alterations; that new and extensive powers ought to be granted to the national head, and that these require a different organization of the federal government, a single body being an unsafe depository of such ample authorities. In conceding all this, the question of expence must be given up, for it is impossible, with any degree of safety, to narrow the foundation upon which the system is to stand. The two branches of the legislature are in the first instance, to consist of only sixty-five persons, which is the same number of which congress, under the existing confederation, may be composed. It is true that this number is intended to be increased; but this is to keep pace with the increase of the population and resources of

---

* *Vide Rutherford's Institutes, vol. 2. book II, chap. x. sect. xiv, and xv. Vide also Grotius, book II, chap. ix, sect. viii, and ix. (Publius)*

the country. It is evident, that a less number would, even in the first instance, have been unsafe; and that a continuance of the present number would, in a more advanced stage of population, be a very inadequate representation of the people.

Whence is the dreaded augmentation of expence to spring? One source pointed out, is the multiplication of offices under the new government. Let us examine this a little.

It is evident that the principal departments of the administration under the present government, are the same which will be required under the new. There are now a secretary at war, a secretary for foreign affairs, a secretary for domestic affairs, a board of treasury consisting of three persons, a treasurer, assistants, clerks, &c. These offices are indispensable under any system, and will suffice under the new as well as under the old. As to ambassadors and other ministers and agents in foreign countries, the proposed constitution can make no other difference, than to render their characters, where they reside, more respectable, and their services more useful. As to persons to be employed in the collection of the revenues, it is unquestionably true that these will form a very considerable addition to the number of federal officers; but it will not follow, that this will occasion an increase of public expence. It will be in most cases nothing more than an exchange of state officers for national officers. In the collection of all duties, for instance, the persons employed will be wholly of the latter description. The states individually will stand in no need of any for this purpose. What difference can it make in point of expence, to pay officers of the customs appointed by the state, or those appointed by the United States? There is no good reason to suppose, that either the number or the salaries of the latter, will be greater than those of the former.

Where then are we to seek for those additional articles of expence which are to swell the account to the enormous size that has been represented to us? The chief item which occurs to me, respects the support of the judges of the United States. I do not add the president, because there is now a president of congress, whose expences may not be far, if any thing, short of those which will be incurred on account of the president of the United States. The support of the judges will clearly be an extra expence, but to what extent will depend on the particular plan which may be adopted in practice in regard to this matter. But it can upon no reasonable plan amount to a sum which will be an object of material consequence.

Let us now see what there is to counterbalance any extra expences that may attend the establishment of the proposed government. The first thing that presents itself is, that a great part of the business, which now keeps congress sitting through the year, will be transacted by the president. Even the management of foreign negociations will naturally devolve upon him according to general principles concerted with the senate, and subject to their final concurrence. Hence it is evident, that a portion of the year will suffice for the session of both the senate and the house of representatives: We may suppose about a fourth for the latter, and a third or perhaps a half for the former. The extra business of treaties and appointments may give this extra occupation to the senate. From this circumstance we may infer, that until the house of representatives shall be increased greatly beyond its present number, there will be a considerable saving of expence from the difference between the constant session of the present, and the temporary session of the future congress.

But there is another circumstance, of great importance in the view of economy. The business of the United States has hitherto occupied the state legislatures as well as congress. The latter has made requisitions which the former have had to provide for. Hence it has happened that the sessions of the state legislatures have been protracted greatly beyond what was necessary for the execution of the mere local business of the states. More than half their time has been frequently employed in matters which related to the United States. Now the members who compose the legislatures of the several states amount to two thousand and upwards; which number has hitherto performed what under the new system will be done in the first instance by sixty-five persons, and probably at no future period by above a fourth or a fifth of that number. The congress under the proposed government will do all the business of the United States themselves, without the intervention of the state legislatures, who thenceforth will have only to attend to the affairs of their particular states, and will not have to sit in any proportion as long as they have heretofore done. This difference, in the time of the sessions of the state legislatures, will be all clear gain, and will alone form an article of saving, which may be regarded as an equivalent for any additional objects of expence that may be occasioned by the adoption of the new system.

The result from these observations is, that the sources of additional expence from the establishment

of the proposed constitution are much fewer than may
have been imagined, that they are counterbalanced by
considerable objects of saving, and that while it is
questionable on which side the scale will preponderate,
it is certain that a government less expensive would be
incompetent to the purposes of the union.

PUBLIUS.

THE FEDERALIST NO. 85

ALEXANDER HAMILTON

MAY 28, 1788

According to the formal division of the subject of these
papers, announced in my first number, there would
appear still to remain for discussion, two points, "the
analogy of the proposed government to your own state
constitution," and "the additional security, which its
adoption will afford to republican government, to liberty and to property." But these heads have been so
fully anticipated and exhausted in the progress of the
work, that it would now scarcely be possible to do any
thing more than repeat, in a more dilated form, what
has been heretofore said; which the advanced stage of
the question, and the time already spent upon it conspire to forbid.

It is remarkable, that the resemblance of the plan of
the convention to the act which organizes the government of this state holds, not less with regard to many
of the supposed defects, than to the real excellencies of

the former. Among the pretended defects, are the re-
eligibility of the executive, the want of a council, the
omission of a formal bill of rights, the omission of a
provision respecting the liberty of the press: These and
several others, which have been noted in the course of
our inquiries, are as much chargeable on the existing
constitution of this state, as on the one proposed for
the Union. And a man must have slender pretensions
to consistency, who can rail at the latter for imperfections which he finds no difficulty in excusing in the
former. Nor indeed can there be a better proof of the
insincerity and affectation of some of the zealous adversaries of the plan of the convention among us, who
profess to be the devoted admirers of the government under which they live, than the fury with which
they have attacked that plan, for matters in regard to
which our own constitution is equally, or perhaps more
vulnerable.

The additional securities to republican government,
to liberty and to property, to be derived from the adoption of the plan under consideration, consist chiefly
in the restraints which the preservation of the union
will impose on local factions and insurrections, and on
the ambition of powerful individuals in single states,
who might acquire credit and influence enough, from
leaders and favorites, to become the despots of the
people; in the diminution of the opportunities to foreign intrigue, which the dissolution of the confederacy
would invite and facilitate; in the prevention of extensive military establishments, which could not fail to
grow out of wars between the states in a disunited
situation; in the express guarantee of a republican form
of government to each; in the absolute and universal

exclusion of titles of nobility; and in the precautions against the repetition of those practices on the part of the state governments, which have undermined the foundations of property and credit, have planted mutual distrust in the breasts of all classes of citizens, and have occasioned an almost universal prostration of morals.

Thus have I, my fellow citizens, executed the task I had assigned to myself; with what success, your conduct must determine. I trust at least you will admit, that I have not failed in the assurance I gave you respecting the spirit with which my endeavours should be conducted. I have addressed myself purely to your judgments, and have studiously avoided those asperities which are too apt to disgrace political disputants of all parties, and which have been not a little provoked by the language and conduct of the opponents of the constitution. The charge of a conspiracy against the liberties of the people, which has been indiscriminately brought against the advocates of the plan, has something in it too wanton and too malignant not to excite the indignation of every man who feels in his own bosom a refutation of the calumny. The perpetual charges which have been rung upon the wealthy, the well-born and the great, have been such as to inspire the disgust of all sensible men. And the unwarrantable concealments and misrepresentations which have been in various ways practiced to keep the truth from the public eye, have been of a nature to demand the reprobation of all honest men. It is not impossible that these circumstances may have occasionally betrayed me into intemperances of expression which I did not intend: It is certain that I have frequently felt a struggle between sensibility and moderation, and if the former has in some instances prevailed, it must be my excuse that it has been neither often nor much.

Let us now pause and ask ourselves whether, in the course of these papers, the proposed constitution has not been satisfactorily vindicated from the aspersions thrown upon it, and whether it has not been shewn to be worthy of the public approbation, and necessary to the public safety and prosperity. Every man is bound to answer these questions to himself, according to the best of his conscience and understanding, and to act agreeably to the genuine and sober dictates of his judgment. This is a duty, from which nothing can give him a dispensation. 'Tis one that he is called upon, nay, constrained by all the obligations that form the bands of society, to discharge sincerely and honestly. No partial motive, no particular interest, no pride of opinion, no temporary passion or prejudice, will justify to himself, to his country or to his posterity, an improper election of the part he is to act. Let him beware of an obstinate adherence to party. Let him reflect that the object upon which he is to decide is not a particular interest of the community, but the very existence of the nation. And let him remember that a majority of America has already given its sanction to the plan, which he is to approve or reject.

I shall not dissemble, that I feel an intire confidence in the arguments, which recommend the proposed system to your adoption; and that I am unable to discern any real force in those by which it has been opposed. I am persuaded, that it is the best which our political situation, habits and opinions will admit, and superior to any the revolution has produced.

Concessions on the part of the friends of the plan, that it has not a claim to absolute perfection, have afforded matter of no small triumph to its enemies. Why, say they, should we adopt an imperfect thing? Why not amend it, and make it perfect before it is irrevocably established? This may be plausible enough, but it is only plausible. In the first place I remark, that the extent of these concessions has been greatly exaggerated. They have been stated as amounting to an admission, that the plan is radically defective; and that, without material alterations, the rights and the interests of the community cannot be safely confided to it. This, as far as I have understood the meaning of those who make the concessions, is an intire perversion of their sense. No advocate of the measure can be found who will not declare as his sentiment, that the system, though it may not be perfect in every part, is upon the whole a good one, is the best that the present views and circumstances of the country will permit, and is such an one as promises every species of security which a reasonable people can desire.

I answer in the next place, that I should esteem it the extreme of imprudence to prolong the precarious state of our national affairs, and to expose the union to the jeopardy of successive experiments, in the chimerical pursuit of a perfect plan. I never expect to see a perfect work from imperfect man. The result of the deliberations of all collective bodies must necessarily be a compound as well of the errors and prejudices, as of the good sense and wisdom of the individuals of whom they are composed. The compacts which are to embrace thirteen distinct states, in a common bond of amity and union, must as necessarily be a compromise of as many dissimilar interests and inclinations. How can perfection spring from such materials?

The reasons assigned in an excellent little pamphlet lately published in this city* are unanswerable to shew the utter improbability of assembling a new convention, under circumstances in any degree so favourable to a happy issue, as those in which the late convention met, deliberated and concluded. I will not repeat the arguments there used, as I presume the production itself has had an extensive circulation. It is certainly well worthy the perusal of every friend to his country. There is however one point of light in which the subject of amendments still remains to be considered; and in which it has not yet been exhibited to public view. I cannot resolve to conclude, without first taking a survey of it in this aspect.

It appears to me susceptible of absolute demonstration, that it will be far more easy to obtain subsequent than previous amendments to the constitution. The moment an alteration is made in the present plan, it becomes, to the purpose of adoption, a new one, and must undergo a new decision of each state. To its complete establishment throughout the union, it will therefore require the concurrence of thirteen states. If, on the contrary, the constitution proposed should once be ratified by all the states as it stands, alterations in it may at any time be effected by nine states. Here then the chances are as thirteen to nine† in favour of subse-

---

* Intitled "An Address to the people of the state of New-York." (Publius)
† It may rather be said TEN, for though two-thirds may set on foot the measure, three-fourths must ratify. (Publius)

quent amendments, rather than of the original adoption of an intire system.

This is not all. Every constitution for the United States must inevitably consist of a great variety of particulars, in which thirteen independent states are to be accommodated in their interests or opinions of interest. We may of course expect to see, in any body of men charged with its original formation, very different combinations of the parts upon different points. Many of those who form the majority on one question may become the minority on a second, and an association dissimilar to either may constitute the majority on a third. Hence the necessity of moulding and arranging all the particulars which are to compose the whole in such a manner as to satisfy all the parties to the compact; and hence also an immense multiplication of difficulties and casualties in obtaining the collective assent to a final act. The degree of that multiplication must evidently be in a ratio to the number of particulars and the number of parties.

But every amendment to the constitution, if once established, would be a single proposition, and might be brought forward singly. There would then be no necessity for management or compromise, in relation to any other point, no giving nor taking. The will of the requisite number would at once bring the matter to a decisive issue. And consequently whenever nine or rather ten states, were united in the desire of a particular amendment, that amendment must infallibly take place. There can therefore be no comparison between the facility of effecting an amendment, and that of establishing in the first instance a complete constitution.

In opposition to the probability of subsequent amendments it has been urged, that the persons delegated to the administration of the national government, will always be disinclined to yield up any portion of the authority of which they were once possessed. For my own part I acknowledge a thorough conviction that any amendments which may, upon mature consideration, be thought useful, will be applicable to the organization of the government, not to the mass of its powers; and on this account alone, I think there is no weight in the observation just stated. I also think there is little weight in it on another account. The intrinsic difficulty of governing THIRTEEN STATES at any rate, independent of calculations upon an ordinary degree of public spirit and integrity, will, in my opinion, constantly *impose* on the national rulers the *necessity* of a spirit of accommodation to the reasonable expectations of their constituents. But there is yet a further consideration, which proves beyond the possibility of doubt, that the observation is futile. It is this, that the national rulers, whenever nine states concur, will have no option upon the subject. By the fifth article of the plan the congress will be *obliged*, "on the application of the legislatures of two-thirds of the states, (which at present amounts to nine) to call a convention for proposing amendments, which *shall be valid* to all intents and purposes, as part of the constitution, when ratified by the legislatures of three-fourths of the states, or by conventions in three-fourths thereof." The words of this article are peremptory. The congress "*shall* call a convention." Nothing in this particular is left to the discretion of that body. And of consequence all the declamation about their disinclination to a change, vanishes in air. Nor however difficult it may be supposed to unite two-thirds or three-fourths of the state legislatures, in amendments which may affect local interests, can there be any room to apprehend any such difficulty in a union on points which are merely relative to the general liberty or security of the people. We may safely rely on the disposition of the state legislatures to erect barriers against the encroachments of the national authority.

If the foregoing argument is a fallacy, certain it is that I am myself deceived by it; for it is, in my conception, one of those rare instances in which a political truth can be brought to the test of mathematical demonstration. Those who see the matter in the same light with me, however zealous they may be for amendments, must agree in the propriety of a previous adoption, as the most direct road to their own object.

The zeal for attempts to amend, prior to the establishment of the constitution, must abate in every man, who, is ready to accede to the truth of the following observations of a writer, equally solid and ingenious: "To balance a large state or society (says he) whether monarchial or republican, on general laws, is a work of so great difficulty, that no human genius, however comprehensive, is able by the mere dint of reason and reflection, to effect it. The judgments of many must unite in the work: EXPERIENCE must guide their labour: TIME must bring it to perfection: And the FEELING of inconveniences must correct the mistakes which they *inevitably* fall into, in their first trials and experiments."* These judicious reflections contain a

---

* Hume's Essays, vol. I, page 128.—*The rise of arts and sciences.* (Publius)

lesson of moderation to all the sincere lovers of the union, and ought to put them upon their guard against hazarding anarchy, civil war, a perpetual alienation of the states from each other, and perhaps the military despotism of a victorious demagogue, in the pursuit of what they are not likely to obtain, but from TIME and EXPERIENCE. It may be in me a defect of political fortitude, but I acknowledge, that I cannot entertain an equal tranquillity with those who affect to treat the dangers of a longer continuance in our present situation as imaginary. A NATION without a NATIONAL GOVERMENT is, in my view, an awful spectacle. The establishment of a constitution, in time of profound peace, by the voluntary consent of a whole people, is a PRODIGY, to the completion of which I look forward with trembling anxiety. I can reconcile it to no rules of prudence to let go the hold we now have, in so arduous an enterprise, upon seven out of the thirteen states; and after having passed over so considerable a part of the ground to recommence the course. I dread the more the consequences of new attempts, because I KNOW that POWERFUL INDIVIDUALS, in this and in other states, are enemies to a general national government, in every possible shape.

PUBLIUS.

■ ||||||||||||||||||||||||||||||||||||||||| ■

Cover art for the Penguin Civic Classics series draws from early American ephemera and was initially inspired by Benjamin Franklin's "Join, or Die" political cartoon, a woodcut print of a divided snake first published in the *Pennsylvania Gazette* in 1754 to stress the importance of colonial unity. Reinterpreted in modern graphic style, these evocative images and symbols have continued to provoke and inspire into the present day.

———•◆•———

The text is set primarily in Adobe Caslon, a version of which was used extensively throughout America's colonial period. Indeed, the first printings of the Declaration of Independence and the Constitution were printed in Caslon.